2020 NOT-FOR-PROFIT ACCOUNTING AND AUDITING UPDATE

BY MELISA F. GALASSO, CPA

T0338194

Notice to readers

2020 Not-for-Profit Accounting and Auditing Update is intended solely for use in continuing professional education and not as a reference. It does not represent an official position of the Association of International Certified Professional Accountants, and it is distributed with the understanding that the author and publisher are not rendering legal, accounting, or other professional services in the publication. This course is intended to be an overview of the topics discussed within, and the author has made every attempt to verify the completeness and accuracy of the information herein. However, neither the author nor publisher can guarantee the applicability of the information found herein. If legal advice or other expert assistance is required, the services of a competent professional should be sought.

You can qualify to earn free CPE through our pilot testing program.
If interested, please visit https://aicpacompliance.polldaddy.com/s/pilot-testing-survey.

ISBN 978-1-11974-720-8 (Paper)
ISBN 978-1-11974-731-4 (ePDF)
ISBN 978-1-11974-730-7 (ePub)
ISBN 978-1-11974-732-1 (oBook)

CL4NAU GS-0420-0A
Revised: **April 2020**

V10018986_060820

Table of Contents

Chapter 1

AICPA Activities

Learning objectives

- Identify the requirements of recently issued Statements on Auditing Standards (SASs).

- Identify common audit deficiencies found by the AICPA.

> The AICPA's Center for Plain English (CPEA) is available to AICPA members that are also members of the Firm Practice Management section (PCPS). The AICPA intends the CPEA to act as a "national office" for small- and medium-sized CPA firms providing accounting and auditing services.

Recently issued auditing and attestation standards

Overview

The Auditing Standards Board (ASB) has recently issued the following SASs and Statements on Standards for Attestation Engagements (SSAEs):

- SAS No. 134, *Auditor Reporting and Amendments, Including Amendments Addressing Disclosures in the Audit of Financial Statements*
- SAS No. 135, *Omnibus Statement of Auditiing Standards – 2019*
- SAS No. 136, *Forming an Opinion and Reporting on Financial Statements of*
- *Employee Benefit Plans Subject to ERISA* (due to nature of topic this will not be addressed in this course)
- SAS No. 137, *The Auditor's Responsibilities Relating to Other Information Included in Annual Reports*
- SAS No. 138, *Amendments to the Description of the Concept of Materiality*
- SSAE No. 19, *Agreed-Upon Procedures Engagements*
- SSAE No. 20, *Amendments to the Description of the Concept of Materiality*

Statements on Auditing Standards

SAS No. 134

Background

SAS No. 134 contains the following four sections:

- AU-C section[1] 700, *Forming an Opinion and Reporting on Financial Statements*
- AU-C section 701 (new), *Communicating Key Audit Matters in the Independent Auditor's Report*
- AU-C section 705, *Modifications to the Opinion in the Independent Auditor's Report*
- AU-C section 706, *Emphasis-of-Matter Paragraphs and Other-Matter Paragraphs in the Independent Auditor's Report*

The ASB considered other standard setters, including the IAASB and PCAOB, in updating the auditor's report. In sticking to its goal of convergence where possible, the ASB decided to converge with the IAASB auditor's report model. Because both the IAASB and PCAOB made formatting changes, the AICPA made changes to the auditor's report to be consistent with changes made with other standard setters.

In keeping with its strategy of convergence, the ASB has considered the revisions to the auditor's report resulting from the IAASB and PCAOB auditor reporting projects in developing the changes to generally accepted auditing standards (GAAS) in SAS No. 134. The ASB believes these changes will increase the

---

[1] All AU-C sections can be found in AICPA *Professional Standards*.

informational value and relevance of the auditor's report for users and, therefore, are in the public interest.

Feedback from user groups informed the changes to the auditor's report. Many users like the current pass-fail model. However, users also indicated that they would appreciate more information about significant aspects of audit procedures and results. Feedback indicated that providing audit specific information would be valuable to users by adding transparency into the audit process.

The following AU-C sections are being superseded:

- AU-C section 700, *Forming an Opinion and Reporting on Financial Statements*
- AU-C section 705, *Modifications to the Opinion in the Independent Auditor's Report,* as amended
- AU-C section 706, *Modifications to the Opinion in the Independent Auditor's Report*

As previously mentioned, a new section is being created: AU-C section 701.

Each section of SAS No. 134 is effective for audits of financial statements for periods ending on or after December 15, 2020. Early implementation is **not** permitted.

AU-C section 700, Forming an opinion and reporting on financial statements

Format

Most users of the audit report will notice that the report has been reorganized. The first header in the new report will be the "Opinion" header. The opinion section will be followed by a "Basis of Opinion" section. Prior to this standard, a basis of opinion paragraph was only added when there was a modification to the opinion. Going forward, all reports will contain a basis of opinion paragraph.

Opinion:

The "Opinion" section starts with the same opening paragraph as previously; auditors will continue to identify the client, the financial statements, and the dates under audit. The second paragraph in the opinion section will present the opinion. The content of this paragraph has not been modified by the new guidance.

The objective of the change is to help the user understand the financial statements better by first stating the conclusion and then explaining how the auditor got there.

> ### Report on the audit of the financial statements[2]
>
> #### Opinion
> We have audited the financial statements of XYZ Not-for-Profit Organization, which comprise the statements of financial position as of December 31, 20X1 and 20X0, and the related statements of activities and cash flows for the years then ended, and the related notes to the financial statements.
>
> In our opinion, the accompanying financial statements present fairly, in all material respects, the financial position of XYZ Not-for-Profit Organization as of December 31, 20X1 and 20X0, and the changes in its net assets and its cash flows for the years then ended in accordance with accounting principles generally accepted in the United States of America.

Basis for opinion

The next section is the "Basis for Opinion" paragraph. The paragraph begins with the same sentence currently in the "Auditor's Responsibility" paragraph indicating that the audit was conducted in accordance with GAAS. After this sentence, two new statements have been added. The first addresses the auditor's responsibilities and refers readers to that section. The other is an explicit statement regarding independence and ethics. Previously, the only mention of independence in the auditor's report was in the report title.

---

[2] The subtitle "Report on the Audit of the Financial Statements" is unnecessary in circumstances in which the second subtitle, "Report on Other Legal and Regulatory Requirements," is not applicable.

> ### Basis for opinion
>
> We conducted our audits in accordance with auditing standards generally accepted in the United States of America (GAAS). Our responsibilities under those standards are further described in the Auditor's Responsibilities for the Audit of the Financial Statements section of our report. We are required to be independent of XYZ Not-for-Profit Organization and to meet our other ethical responsibilities, in accordance with the relevant ethical requirements relating to our audits. We believe that the audit evidence we have obtained is sufficient and appropriate to provide a basis for our audit opinion.

Although the "Opinion" section is required to be first in the report, followed by the "Basis of Opinion" section, the new report otherwise provides a lot of flexibility in the reporting and order of paragraphs. This course covers the basic paragraphs. However, "Emphasis-of-Matter," "Other-Matter," and "Key Audit Matters" paragraphs have flexibility in placement and prioritization.

Responsibilities of management

The next section is the "Responsibilities of Management for the Financial Statements" paragraph in a report with no modifications, key audit matters (KAM) or emphasis paragraphs. The section includes much of the current language for management including responsibility for preparation and fair presentation as well as design, implementation, and maintenance of internal controls. There is an added focus, however, on management's responsibility to evaluate the entity's ability to continue as a going concern when that is required by the financial reporting framework used by the client.

> ### Responsibilities of management and those charged with governance for the financial statements
>
> Management is responsible for the preparation and fair presentation of the financial statements in accordance with accounting principles generally accepted in the United States of America, and for the design, implementation, and maintenance of internal control relevant to the preparation and fair presentation of financial statements that are free from material misstatement, whether due to fraud or error.
>
> In preparing the financial statements, management is required to evaluate whether there are conditions or events, considered in the aggregate, that raise substantial doubt about XYZ Not-for-Profit Organization ability to continue as a going concern for [*insert the time period set by the applicable financial reporting framework*].

Auditor's responsibilities

The next section highlights the auditor's responsibilities for an audit. Significantly expanded, this section walks the users through the process of performing an audit from start to finish. In lieu of focus on responsibilities the way the prior report format did, the new report focuses on the auditor's objectives similar to the language used in the SAS. The opening paragraph adds a definition of reasonable assurance as well as of material misstatement; this is to assist the users of the financial statements with interpreting the language used to explain the role of the auditor. The report also discusses the use of professional judgment and professional skepticism.

The largest portion of this section focuses the reader on the process of performing an audit. It explains the role of risk assessment (see AU-C section 315, *Understanding the Entity and Its Environment and Assessing the Risks of Material Misstatement*), response to risk (see AU-C section 330, *Performing Audit Procedures in Response to Assessed Risks and Evaluating the Audit Evidence Obtained*), and audit evidence (see AU-C section 500, *Audit Evidence*). The section also addresses the fact that fraud is harder to detect than material misstatement. The standard calls attention to issues like collusion and override of internal controls that limit the effectiveness of internal controls and make it harder for auditors to find fraud. Also covered is the role of internal controls with similar language that has been used by auditors to communicate a focus on obtaining an understanding of internal control to enable the design of appropriate procedures. It also addresses the responsibilities for estimate made by management similar to the current auditor's report. There is new language regarding going concern depending on the financial reporting framework used. Finally, the section addresses communications with those charged with governance. The section uses bullet points as a means of communicating the various responsibilities.

Note: SAS No. 138 updates the definition of materiality. As such, this section was updated to reflect the updated definition.

> ### Auditor's responsibilities for the audit of the financial statements
>
> Our objectives are to obtain reasonable assurance about whether the financial statements as a whole are free from material misstatement, whether due to fraud or error, and to issue an auditor's report that includes our opinion. Reasonable assurance is a high level of assurance but is not absolute assurance and therefore is not a guarantee that an audit conducted in accordance with GAAS will always detect a material misstatement when it exists. The risk of not detecting a material misstatement resulting from fraud is higher than for one resulting from error, as fraud may involve collusion, forgery, intentional omissions, misrepresentations, or the override of internal control. Misstatements are considered material if there is a substantial likelihood that, individually or in the aggregate, they would influence the judgment made by a reasonable user based on the financial statements.
>
> In performing an audit in accordance with GAAS, we:
>
> - Exercise professional judgment and maintain professional skepticism throughout the audit.
> - Identify and assess the risks of material misstatement of the financial statements, whether due to fraud or error, and design and perform audit procedures responsive to those risks. Such procedures include examining, on a test basis, evidence regarding the amounts and disclosures in the financial statements.

> **Auditor's responsibilities for the audit of the financial statements (continued)**
>
> - Obtain an understanding of internal control relevant to the audit in order to design audit procedures that are appropriate in the circumstances, but not for the purpose of expressing an opinion on the effectiveness of XYZ Not-for-Profit Organization's internal control. Accordingly, no such opinion is expressed.[3]
> - Evaluate the appropriateness of accounting policies used and the reasonableness of significant accounting estimates made by management, as well as evaluate the overall presentation of the financial statements.
> - Conclude whether, in our judgment, there are conditions or events, considered in the aggregate, that raise substantial doubt about XYZ Not-for-Profit Organization's ability to continue as a going concern for a reasonable period of time.
>
> We are required to communicate with those charged with governance regarding, among other matters, the planned scope and timing of the audit, significant audit findings, and certain internal control related matters that we identified during the audit.

Now that the "Opinion" section has been moved to the top of the report, the final required paragraph would be the "Auditor's Responsibilities for the Audit of the Financial Statements" section. If the auditor has any other reporting responsibilities for the engagement, this would be disclosed directly after the "Auditor's Responsibilities" section in the "Report on Other Legal and Regulatory Requirements" section. The signature of the auditor, the city and state, and the date of the report would then appear at the bottom.

See an example auditor's report in appendix B of this chapter.

Knowledge check

1. What is the first section heading in the new auditor's report?

    a. Opinion.
    b. Basis for Opinion.
    c. Management's Responsibilities.
    d. Auditor's Responsibilities for the Audit of the Financial Statements.

AU-C section 701, Communicating key audit matters in the Independent Auditor's Report

AU-C section 701 introduces the concept of key audit matters (KAM). The IAASB requires the reporting of KAM for listed entities (comparable to issuers in the United States) and PCAOB has a similar concept called critical audit matters that is required. The AICPA decided not to require the communication of KAM for all entities. Instead, the auditor is only required to report KAM if they are specifically engaged to

---

[3] In circumstances in which the auditor also has a responsibility to express an opinion on the effectiveness of internal control in conjunction with the audit of the financial statements, omit the following: "but not for the purpose of expressing an opinion on the effectiveness of XYZ Not-for-Profit Organization's internal control. Accordingly, no such opinion is expressed."

communicate KAM. Potential reasons an auditor may be engaged to report KAM include requirements by regulators, banks, or parent companies who request KAM. When the auditor is engaged to communicate KAM, the auditor is required to apply AU-C section 701.

Definition:

Key audit matters, or KAM are those matters that, in the auditor's **professional judgment**, were of **most significance** in the audit of the financial statements of the **current period**. Key audit matters are selected from matters **communicated with those charged with governance**.

The scope of KAM guidance applies only to audits of complete sets of general-purpose financial statements. Auditors are prohibited from reporting KAM when issuing an adverse or disclaimer of opinion, unless the reporting is required by law or regulation.

As noted in the definition, KAM are matters that were of most significance in the audit. Significance is typically considered by using a risk based approach to auditing. Typically, the higher the risk, the more attention is given in planning and the more extensive the required procedures. Significant risks that require special audit responses would likely be considered for determination as to whether they required significant attention. However, not all significant risks are KAM. Auditors will need to identify areas that posed challenges during the audit and perhaps required consultation or the use of a specialist. Other areas, such as estimates with high estimation uncertainty and related party transactions, are also considerations for KAM.

The population for KAM selection is topics that were **communicated to those charged with governance.** AU-C section 260, *Auditor's Communication With Those Charged With Governance*, requires communication of significant difficulties encountered during the audit, related party transactions, and matters related to group audits. AU-C section 220, *Quality Control for an Engagement Conducted in Accordance With Generally Accepted Auditing Standards*, provides required communication regarding consultation on difficult or contentious matters and AU-C section 265, *Communicating Internal Control Related Matters Identified in and Audit*, provides guidance on communicating internal control deficiencies.

The population for KAM could potentially be quite large. However, the auditor is required to select those that are of the "most significance" which requires the auditor to rank the items. Considerations include the importance to users, the nature of underlying accounting policy, nature and materiality of corrected and uncorrected misstatements, nature and extent of audit effort, nature and severity of difficulties in applying audit procedures, and severity of control deficiencies in trying to determine a relative significance. The largest area of professional judgement is determining ultimately what and how many were most significant. The number of items ultimately determined to be KAM is affected by size and complexity of entity, nature of business and environment, and facts and circumstances of audit engagement.

Once KAM is identified, there will be a separate section of the auditor's report with a heading titled, "Key Audit Matters." The section starts with a required introductory paragraph to introduce the concept of KAM and how KAM fits in with the overall audit's objectives.

"Key audit matters are those matters that were communicated with those charged with governance and, in the auditor's professional judgment, were of most significance in the audit of the financial statements [of the current period]. These matters were addressed in the context of the audit of the financial statements as a whole, and in forming the auditor's opinion thereon, and the auditor does not provide a separate opinion on these matters."

In the following paragraphs within the section, the auditor describes each KAM, includes a reference to related disclosures as appropriate, and describes why the matter was considered to be one of the most significant in the audit. In addition, the auditor discloses how the matter was addressed in the audit. The auditor, using professional judgment, determines the amount of detail. Examples of how to describe how the matter was addressed may include an overview of procedures performed and/or an indication of the outcome of procedures (without implying a discrete opinion on separate elements of the financial statements). The goal is to meet financial statement user needs by providing entity specific information that is not overly standardized or boilerplate.

Laws and regulations could potentially preclude the disclosure of a particular matter. Similar to Yellow Book, the auditor would have to determine the appropriate response. Auditors also determine whether any adverse consequences of reporting the matter would reasonably be expected to outweigh public interest benefits of such communication, keeping in mind the goal of KAM is transparency. Management's views about adverse consequences do not alleviate the need for auditor determined cost-benefit analysis.

The following items are required documentation items:

- The matters that required significant auditor attention
- Rationale for whether or not each of the matters is a KAM
- Reason a KAM was not communicated in auditor's report

Auditors are not required to document why other matters communicated with those charged with governance were not matters that required significant auditor attention.

AU-C section 705, Modifications to the Opinion in the Independent Auditor's Report

AU-C section 705 provides examples of audit reports when modifying the auditor's opinion. When issuing a qualified opinion, a second paragraph is added to the basis for opinion section providing an explanation of the cause of the modification. This is similar to the use of the basis paragraph prior to SAS No. 134. A similar paragraph is added when providing an adverse opinion. However, a disclaimer opinion looks very unique. The standard continues to use the concept of "we were engaged" instead of "we have audited." The second paragraph continues to indicate "we do not express an opinion." However, the standard basis of opinion paragraph is removed and only the paragraph related to the reason for disclaiming an opinion is reported. In addition, the auditor's responsibility paragraph is shortened to two paragraphs. The first is a very shortened discussion of the auditor's responsibilities. The second and final sentence in the first paragraph explains that because of the item described in the basis paragraph the auditor did not obtain sufficient appropriate evidence. The verbiage about reasonable assurance, material misstatement etc. are removed from the paragraph. The bulleted list of audit procedures is also removed. Instead the section closes with the statement of independence normally found in the basis paragraph. A user will easily be able to determine that this is not a normal clean opinion just from the length of the report.

AU-C section 706, Emphasis-of-Matter Paragraphs and Other-Matter Paragraphs in the Independent Auditor's Report

AU-C section 706 addresses emphasis of matter and other matter paragraphs. Both definitions are updated to describe the interplay with the concept of KAM. The section also provides guidance on placement of EOM and OM paragraphs and their interaction with KAM paragraphs. Reporting on annual reports and going concern paragraphs are no longer deemed to be emphasis or other matter paragraphs. Instead they are separate sections under SAS No. 134.

Knowledge check

2. When issuing a qualified opinion, how many paragraphs would the basis for opinion paragraph have?

    a. 0
    b. 1
    c. 2
    d. 3

Other Changes

While the focus of SAS No. 134 is the changes to the auditor's report, there are also two other types of changes – conforming amendments and changes made due to the disclosure project. As evidenced by the title, one of the biggest areas of focus outside of the report was the consideration of the auditor of disclosures throughout the audit. The standard moves the terminology towards the use of disclosures instead of the term notes. Changes to AU-C 200 provides more guidance on what is a disclosure and its purpose. AU-C 210 is also updated to include changes to the engagement letter to reflect the new report language. AU-C 240 includes a focus on the consideration of fraud to note disclosures and adds that omitting, obscuring, or misstating disclosures is a characteristic of fraud. In the discussion among team members, the standard adds a discussion regarding disclosures that obscure understanding by being unclear or ambiguous. AU-C 260 adds communications regarding significant risks during the planning phase and includes additional communication considerations for communication with those charged with governance. AU-C 300 focuses on the audit plan related to disclosures while adding considerations in planning regarding disclosures. AU-C 315 incorporates additional risk assessment considerations for disclosures. Another key change is that assertions related to presentation and disclosures were removed and instead incorporated at the account balance and class of transaction level. AU-C 330 addresses misstatements related to inappropriate classification and omissions of disclosures. AU-C 600 provides updated reporting for group audits. As a result, auditors should carefully review checklists, audit programs and communications to ensure compliance when adopting SAS No. 134.

Future changes

The AICPA has issued multiple exposure drafts to update all sections impacted by the audit report changes. This includes *Proposed Statement on Auditing Standards, Amendments to AU-C sections 800, 805, and 810 to Incorporate Auditor Reporting Changes From SAS No. 134 and Proposed Statement on Auditing Standards, Amendments to AU-C sections 725, 730, 930, 935, and 940.* As of January 2020, these changes were in the proposal phase.

> You are encouraged to monitor the changes to these sections at aicpa.org.

Knowledge check

3. AU-C section 701 introduces what new section of the audit report?

    a. Key audit matters.
    b. Critical audit matters.
    c. Significant audit matters.
    d. Crucial audit matters.

SAS No. 135

SAS No. 135 was issued in April 2019 and is effective for audits of financial statements for periods ending on or after December 15, 2020.

When the AICPA last overhauled the audit standards back in 2012 as part of the Clarity Project, the focus was on convergence with the IAASB, but also considered were opportunities to converge with the PCAOB. Since the Clarity Standards, the PCAOB has issued the following:

- AS 1301, *Communication with Audit Committees*
- AS 2701, Supplementary Information
- AS 2410, *Related Parties*

As a result, the AICPA reviewed the changes to determine where it would make sense to converge GAAS with PCAOB standards.

The new standard addresses an entity's significant unusual transactions, potential effects of uncorrected misstatements on future-period financial statements, and consultations with those outside the engagement team.

To clarify current GAAS, the new standard consistently uses the term *significant unusual transactions*, which are "significant transactions that are outside the normal course of business for the entity or that otherwise appear to be unusual due to their timing, size or nature."

The new standard also enhances requirements to identify previously unidentified or undisclosed related parties or significant related party transactions and enhances the response to the risk of material misstatement associated with related parties.

The AICPA decided no amendments were necessary to converge with AS 2701, which deals primarily with broker-dealers.

Knowledge check

4. Which AS standard issued by the PCAOB was addressed in new SAS No. 135?

    a. AS 1301.
    b. AS 2701.
    c. AS 1005.
    d. AS 2570.

SAS No. 137

SAS No. 137, *The Auditor's Responsibilities Relating to Other Information Included in Annual Reports*, was issued in July 2019 and is effective for audits of financial statements for periods ending on or after December 15, 2020. Upon its effective date, it will supersede the extant AU-C section 720, *Other Information in Documents Containing Audited Financial Statements.*

This project also stemmed out of the ASB's strategy to converge the SASs with the ISAs while tailoring to the U.S. environment. The standard provides guidance on the auditor's responsibilities when the auditor's report and audited financial statements are included in documents containing other information (OI). For purposes of the standard, OI is limited to annual reports, and a new definition of an annual report is provided.

> **Annual report.** A document, or combination of documents, typically prepared on an annual basis by management or those charged with governance in accordance with law, regulation, or custom, the purpose of which is to provide owners (or similar stakeholders) with information on the entity's operations and the entity's financial results and financial position as set out in the financial statements. An annual report contains, accompanies, or incorporates by reference the financial statements and the auditor's report thereon and usually includes information about the entity's developments, its future outlook and risks and uncertainties, a statement by the entity's governing body, and reports covering governance matters. Annual reports include annual reports of governments and organizations for charitable or philanthropic purposes that are available to the public.

Even if a document is called an annual report, unless it meets the definition of an annual report, it is not in the scope of this proposed standard. OI is different from required supplementary information (see AU-C section 730, Required Supplementary Information) and supplementary information (see AU-C section 725, Supplementary Information in Relation to the Financial Statements as a Whole).

Examples of items that do not qualify as annual reports include IRS Form 990, *Return of Organization Exempt From Income Tax* and IRS Form 5500, *Annual Return/Report of Employee Benefit Plan*. However, many nonprofits do issue annual reports for communications to the board and donors. In addition, the updated definition of annual reports of governments is intended to include comprehensive annual financial reports (CAFR) or other annual financial reports that include the government's financial statements and the auditor's report thereon.

When a client issues an annual report the auditor is required to consider whether a material inconsistency exists between the other information and the financial statements. They should also remain alert for indications that a material inconsistency exists between the other information and the auditor's knowledge obtained in the audit or a material misstatement of fact exists or the other information is otherwise misleading . If there is a material inconsistency or error, the auditor must respond appropriately. In addition, if the auditor receives the annual report prior to issuance of the

---

opinion on the financial statements (which is not required), then the auditor would report on the annual report as a separate section in the auditor's report to explain their responsibilities for the annual report.

The auditor's opinion on the financial statements does not cover the other information and the auditor is NOT required to obtain audit evidence beyond that required to form an opinion on the financial statements. Therefore, the primary audit procedures will include reading the annual report and remaining alert for contradictory or incorrect information.

SAS No. 138

SAS No. 138 was issued in December 2019 and addresses the definition of materiality. The original definition of materiality in the United States dates back to a US Supreme Court case. However, during the 2000s both FASB and AICPA decided to converge the definition with international standards. In 2018, FASB after ending its convergence effort reverted back to the original definition of materiality. As such, the AICPA, while still maintaining an active convergence effort, also agreed to update the definition to be more consistent with US standard setters. The largest change is in the concept of could (a hypothetical) to would (a more definitive scenario). The updated definition also incorporates the concept of substantial likelihood and the framework of a reasonable user. SAS No. 138 updates the language in the auditor's report. Conforming amendments are also made to AU-C 200, Overall Objectives of the Independent Auditor and the Conduct of an Audit in Accordance With Generally Accepted Auditing Standards, AU-C 320, Materiality in Planning and Performing an Audit, AU-C 450, Evaluation of Misstatements Identified During the Audit, and AU-C 600, Special Considerations — Audits of Group Financial Statements (Including the Work of Component Auditors).

Knowledge check

5. A key change in the definition of materiality is the word?

    a. is
    b. could
    c. will
    d. for

Statements on Standards for Attestation Engagements

SSAE 19

SSAE 19, *Agreed-Upon Procedures Engagements*, was issued in December 2019. It supersedes SSAE 18, *Attestation Standards: Clarification and Recodification, AT-C section 215, Agreed-Upon Procedures Engagements* and amends SSAE No. 18 AT-C section 105, *Concepts Common to All Attestation Engagements*. The standard addresses many practice issues that have made it difficult for practitioners to comply with the AUP standards. The first thing the standard does is update AT-C 105 to remove the requirement to obtain an assertion in AUPs as sometimes the responsible party may not have the ability or willingness to perform its own measurement or evaluation of the subject matter. Another practice issue addressed is now the CPA, the responsible party, or the engaging party can write the procedures. The prior standard did not permit the CPA to write the procedures for the client. Prior to the issuance of the report, the engaging party is required to agree to and acknowledge that the procedures performed are appropriate to meet the intended purpose of the engagement. As a result, the intended uses are no longer required to take responsibility for the sufficiency of the procedures which was oftentimes difficult to obtain. In addition, AUP reports no longer require restriction and can be issued as general purpose. The report is also updated to incorporate the statement of independence in SAS No. 134. The standard is effective for AUP reports dated on or after July 15, 2021 and early implementation is permitted.

Knowledge check

6. SSAE 19 updates the requirements for which type of attestation engagement?

    a. examination
    b. review
    c. agreed upon procedure
    d. compilation

SSAE 20

SSAE 20, Amendments to the Description of the Concept of Materiality, was issued in December 2019. Similar to SAS No. 138, this standard updates the definition of materiality to be consistent with US Standard Setters. It will be effective for practitioners' examination reports dated on or after December 15, 2020 and practitioners' review reports dated on or after December 15, 2020.

Recently issued changes to the Code of Professional Conduct

Leases

Due to the changes in the definition of a lease and the change in accounting for leases by both GASB and FASB, the AICPA started a project to update the "Leases" interpretation (ET sec. 1.260.040) in the Code of Professional Conduct. The prior standard included exceptions for certain types of leases. Under the new standard, when a CPA enters into or has a lease with an attest client, self-interest, familiarity, and undue influence threats may exist.

If a covered member who is an individual on the attest engagement team, an individual in a position to influence the attest engagement, or the firm enters into a lease or renegotiates terms of an existing lease with an attest client during the period of the professional engagement, threats to compliance with the "Independence Rule" would not be at an acceptable level and could not be reduced to an acceptable level by the application of safeguards.

Independence would be impaired, unless all of the following safeguards are met at the time of entering into or renegotiating the lease:

a. The lease is on market terms and established at arm's length.
b. The lease is not material to any of the parties to the lease. When evaluating materiality, all leases between the covered member and the attest client should be considered in the aggregate.

The covered member must pay the lease amounts in accordance with the lease terms and provisions by the due date to prevent threats to independence.

For existing leases, the covered member should evaluate the significance of any threats to determine whether the threats are at an acceptable level. If the covered member determines that threats are not at an acceptable level, the covered member should apply safeguards to eliminate or reduce the threats to an acceptable level. If no safeguards are available to eliminate or reduce threats to an acceptable level, independence would be impaired.

The "Client Affiliates" interpretation (ET sec. 1.224.010) is now revised to apply for leases held with certain affiliates of a financial statement attest client.

These changes are effective for fiscal years beginning after December 15, 2019.

Information System Services (1.295.145)

In June 2019, the section of the Code of Professional Content formerly known as "Information Systems Design, Implementation, or Integration" was updated. Terminology was refreshed and the standard was made more precise regarding what factors impair independence when a member in public practice assists a client with their information system services. The interpretation applies to all attest engagements, including examinations, agreed upon procedures, and others in which the subject matter of the engagement is not financial statements.

The standard defines a financial information system (FIS) as:

> "a system that aggregates source data underlying the financial statements or generates information that is significant to either the financial statements or financial processes as a whole."

Additional definitions for this standard are as follows:

- "Designing an information system means determining how a system or transaction will function, process data, and produce results (for example, reports, journal vouchers, and documents such as sales and purchase orders) to provide a blueprint or schematic for the development of software code (programs) and data structures."
- "Developing an information system entails creating software code, for individual or multiple modules, and testing such code to confirm it is functioning as designed."

When the project is not related to a financial information system, threats are considered to be at an acceptable level if the CPA performed design, development or implementation services only when the normal nonattest service requirements are met (i.e., client takes responsibility etc.).

The following chart summarizes the rules when a member is performing work on a FIS:

Design	Impairs independence
Develop	Impairs independence
Installing	Follow nonattest service rules
Configure	Follow nonattest service rules
Customize	Impairs independence
Interface	Impairs independence (exception for application programming interfaces)
Translate Data	Impairs independence (exception for application programming interfaces)
Ongoing System and Network Maintenance, Support & Monitoring	Impairs independence
Separate & Distinct System and Network Maintenance, Support & Monitoring	Follow nonattest service rules

This interpretation is effective beginning Jan. 1, 2021. Early implementation is allowed.

Knowledge check

7. Which is a prohibited service?

   a. Use of APIs to translate data
   b. Distinct network support
   c. Developing a FIS
   d. Installing a FIS

State and Local Government Client Affiliates (1.224.020)

Effective for years beginning after December 15, 2020, the new State and Local Government Client Affiliates interpretation was issued in June 2019. While the definition of client affiliate has been used for several years under the Code, PEEC recognizes that governmental entities are different in that the financial reporting entity rolls up at various levels. Therefore, PEEC created a new definition of an affiliate that is unique to governmental entities that follow GASB.

"An affiliate of a financial statement attest client exists in all the following situations:

   i. The entity is included in the financial statement attest client's financial statements and the member or member's firm does not make reference to another auditor's report on the entity.
   ii. The entity is included in the financial statement attest client's financial statements, the member or member's firm makes reference to another auditor's report on the entity, and
       (1) the entity is material to the financial statement attest client's financial statements as a whole and
       (2) the financial statement attest client has more than minimal influence over the entity's accounting or financial reporting process. There is a rebuttable presumption that the financial statement attest client has more than minimal influence over the accounting or financial reporting process of funds and blended component units.
   iii. The entity is a material excluded entity, and the financial statement attest client has more than minimal influence over the entity's accounting or financial reporting process. A material excluded entity is an entity that is required under the applicable financial reporting framework to be included in the financial statements of the financial statement attest client but is, nevertheless, excluded by the financial statement attest client and is material to the financial statement attest client's financial statements as a whole. There is a rebuttable presumption that the financial statement attest client has more than minimal influence over the accounting or financial reporting process of funds and blended component units.
   iv. The investor, which is either the financial statement attest client or an affiliate as defined in item (i) of this definition, has an investment in an investee when the investor either
       (1) controls the investee, unless the investment in the investee is trivial and clearly inconsequential to the financial statement attest client's financial statements as a whole, or
       (2) has significant influence over the investee and the investment in the investee is material to the financial statement attest client's financial statements as a whole."

Threats to independence may arise as a result of financial interests or other relationships with governmental affiliates of a financial statement attest client. The interpretation highlights that other relationships can cause threats to independence, including:

"a   A covered member's immediate family member is in a key position with a nonaffiliate that includes the financial statement attest client in its financial statements and the nonaffiliate provides accounting staff, shares financial information systems, or establishes internal controls over financial reporting for the financial statement attest client.

b.   The member or member's firm is considering providing financial information system design services to a nonaffiliate in which the same financial information system would also be used by the financial statement attest client.

c.   A covered member has a financial interest in a nonaffiliate that includes the financial statement attest client in its financial statements, and the nonaffiliate prepares the financial statements for the financial statement attest client.

d.   The financial statement attest client participates in a public-private partnership or joint venture that does not meet the definition of an investment in paragraph .03c of this interpretation. A covered member has a financial interest in an organization that is also involved with the public-private partnership or joint venture.

e.   A covered member owns utility bonds issued by a nonaffiliate, and the financial statement attest client is responsible for payment of the utility bond debt service.

f.   A covered member owns conduit debt issued by the financial statement attest client on behalf of a nonaffiliate. The conduit debt is not accounted for on the financial statements of the financial statement attest client, and the debt service is paid by the nonaffiliate."

Therefore, going forward, it is important that auditors of governmental entities take the time to properly identify client affiliates and consider any threats to independence – which may be more time intensive due to the way governmental entities prepare financial statements.

PEEC has also issued a three-year plan document on potential future projects which can be found: https://www.aicpa.org/content/dam/aicpa/interestareas/professionalethics/community/downloadabledocuments/peecstrategy-workplan-consultation.pdf

Other projects to monitor

Check the AICPA website at www.aicpa.org to follow the status of the following projects:

- Management's Specialist
- Risk Assessment

ASB exposure drafts are posted to the AICPA's website at
https://www.aicpa.org/research/exposuredrafts/accountingandauditing.html

In 2019, the ASB issued a consultation paper on its strategy and workplan. Information regarding potential projects can be found at:
https://www.aicpa.org/content/dam/aicpa/research/standards/auditattest/asb/downloadabledocuments/asb-strategy-consultation-paper.pdf

2018 mid-year progress report – Enhancing Audit Quality

Background

The AICPA launched its Enhancing Audit Quality (EAQ) Initiative in May 2014 and released a related EAQ discussion paper on August 7, 2014. The EAQ Initiative is a holistic effort to consider auditing of private entities through multiple touch points, especially where quality issues have emerged. The goal is to align the objectives of all audit-related AICPA efforts to improve audit performance.

The EAQ Initiative is a six-point plan to improve audit quality and therefore preserve the prominent and respected role the CPA in public practice plays in the business community. The objective of this program is to improve consistency of quality by focusing the attention of firms and peer reviewers on the following:

- New industries
- Industries with new/rising risks
- Employee benefit plans
- Municipalities
- Audit areas of increased risk
- Documentation of sufficient appropriate audit evidence
- Nonattest services to audit clients
- Areas with increased inspection areas in the past

As part of the Enhancing Audit Quality Initiative, the AICPA issued a document titled "Enhancing Audit Quality: 2017 Highlights and Progress." The document provides insights into the reviews of Single Audits that received enhanced oversight. For all audits (including single audits), 55% of all audits reviewed were materially nonconforming in 2016.

The most common causes of non-conformity were

- inadequate or nonexistent audit documentation,
- no testing of internal controls over compliance in single audits, and
- no testing of one or more applicable compliance requirements in single audits.

The rate of non-conformity with professional standards peer reviewers detected on must-select engagements has more than tripled since 2015. Three percent of firms in the FAC database were not properly enrolled in the peer review program or failed to report to their peer reviewer that they performed a single audit (evaluation performed in 2015–16 for year-ends in 2013).

Twenty-three percent of all single audits subject to enhanced oversight were materially non-conforming with professional standards due to failure to properly test controls over compliance. Sixteen percent of single audits subject to enhanced oversight were materially non-conforming due to failure to properly test direct and material compliance requirements.

The AICPA identified the following three key factors driving single audit quality:

- The more single audits a firm performed every year (regardless of firm size), the more likely a given single audit was to conform to professional standards.
- GAQC membership firm members had two times greater conformity than non-members.
- The number of single audits the engagement partner performed annually

GAQC members who performed 11 or more single audits annually were found to be in conformity 100% of the time. The theme is practice makes perfect, and commitment to quality is key to audit quality success.

Knowledge check

8. For all audits subject to enhanced oversight in 2016, what percent were materially nonconforming?

    a. 25%.
    b. 35%.
    c. 45%.
    d. 55%.

The 2018 EAQ areas of focus were risk assessment, documentation, single audits, auditing in the future, and peer review. In 2018, the AICPA issued a document titled "Enhancing Audit Quality: 2018 mid-year progress report." The document provides updates on five areas, three of which were 2018 areas of focus, as part of the EAQ Initiative.

- Peer review
    - Eighty-six percent of firms improved in their next peer review when the Peer Review Program required a third-party review of their engagements or quality control documents. A 2015 study found that 16% of firms required to subject their employee benefit plan audits to peer review had failed to do so. A 2017 study found that noncompliance had been cut in half.
- Single audits
    - More than 8,600 auditors and organizations subject to single audits learned about single audit resources and the results of a November 2017 study conducted by the AICPA on the factors driving single audit quality.
- Employee benefit plan audits
    - The AICPA presented a webcast in December 2017 titled, "EBP Audits: Common Misconceptions and How to Address Them."
- Quality control
    - There were more than 7,900 quality control resource downloads in 2017, based on more than 4,900 visits to the Private Companies Practice Section's Invigorate the Focus on Quality Toolkit.
- Documentation
    - The progress report noted that more than 50% of all material noncompliance with auditing standards is due to inadequate audit documentation. A quiz to test knowledge of the audit documentation standard was published in *Journal of Accountancy* in 2017 (see the quiz at journalofaccountancy.com/documentation). More than 10,000 people took the quiz. There were more than 15,000 visits to the free audit documentation toolkit at aicpa.org/documentation.

Addressing common audit deficiencies

Lack of documentation

Lack of sufficient documentation in audits has consistently been the number one audit quality issue. One in every 4 engagements (or 25%) subject to enhanced oversite by the Peer Review Program is materially non-conforming because of poor documentation.

Per an article in the *Journal of Accounting* June 2017 issue, interviews with firms subject to enhanced oversight uncovered three common misconceptions that drive nonconformity.

1. Auditors can meet their overall audit objectives without documenting their work.
2. A sign-off on an audit program is sufficient documentation of a detail test.
3. Oral explanation can substitute for written documentation to meet the requirements of AU-C section 230, *Audit Documentation*.

Some of the more common examples where there is frequently lack of documentation include tests of controls over compliance in single audits, direct and material compliance requirement determinations in single audits, eligibility testing in EBP audits, and consideration of systems and organization controls reports.

What is documentation?

Per AU-C section 230, audit documentation is the record of audit procedures performed, relevant audit evidence obtained, and conclusions the auditor reached. The terms *working papers* or *workpapers* are often used synonymously.

Audit documentation must provide evidence of the auditor's basis for a conclusion regarding the overall objective of the audit and evidence that the audit was planned and performed in accordance with GAAS and applicable legal and regulatory requirements.

The auditor should prepare audit documentation that is sufficient to enable an experienced auditor, with no previous connection with the audit, to understand the nature, timing, and extent of the audit procedures performed, the results of those audit procedures and the supporting audit evidence obtained, as well as the audit conclusions reached (including significant findings and issues, and primary professional judgments made in reaching those conclusions).

Audit documentation may be recorded on paper or on electronic media. Preliminary drafts, initial thinking, and incomplete notes do not need to be maintained if they are superseded by a final draft. Additionally, oral explanation may be used to explain or clarify audit documentation, but no amount of oral explanation can substitute for missing or incomplete written documentation.

Why does documentation matter?

AU-C section 200, *Overall Objectives of the Independent Auditor and the Conduct of an Audit in Accordance With Generally Accepted Auditing Standards,* paragraph .19 states that obtaining reasonable assurance requires the auditor to "obtain sufficient appropriate audit evidence to reduce audit risk to an acceptably low level and thereby enable the auditor to draw reasonable conclusions on which to base the auditor's opinion." Obtaining audit evidence requires that work be completed and appropriately documented.

AU-C section 230 further states that the objective of the auditor is to prepare documentation that provides a sufficient and appropriate record of the basis for the auditor's report and evidence that the audit was planned and performed in accordance with GAAS and applicable legal and regulatory requirements.

Audit documentation serves several additional purposes such as the following:

- Assisting the engagement team to plan and perform the audit
- Assisting members of the engagement team responsible for supervision to direct and supervise the audit work and to discharge their review responsibilities in accordance with AU-C section 220
- Enabling the engagement team to demonstrate that it is accountable for its work by documenting the procedures performed, the audit evidence examined, and the conclusions reached
- Retaining a record of matters of continuing significance to future audits of the same entity
- Enabling the conduct of quality control reviews and inspections in accordance with QC section 10, *A Firm's System of Quality Control* (AICPA *Professional Standards*)
- Enabling the conduct of external inspections or peer reviews in accordance with applicable legal, regulatory, or other requirements
- Assisting an auditor who reviews a predecessor auditor's audit documentation
- Assisting auditors to understand the work performed in the prior year as an aid in planning and performing the current engagement

Even in the case of small audits where all work is completed by a sole audit partner, audit documentation must still be prepared in a manner that can be understood by an experienced auditor with no previous knowledge of the engagement for peer review or litigation purposes.

Form, content, and extent of audit documentation

Documentation should be prepared on a timely basis because it helps enhance audit quality, facilitates effective review before an auditor's report is finalized, and increases the likelihood that documentation will be accurate. Additionally, finally assembly of the audit documentation in an audit file should be completed no later than 60 days following the report release date.

As previously noted, audit documentation should be sufficient to enable an experienced auditor, with no previous connection with the audit, to understand the nature, timing, and extent of the audit procedures performed, the results of those audit procedures and the supporting audit evidence obtained, as well as, the audit conclusions reached (including significant findings and issues and primary professional judgments made in reaching those conclusions).

However, the form, content, and extent of audit documentation will depend on several factors including the following:

- Size and complexity of the entity
- Nature of the audit procedures to be performed
- Identified risks of material misstatement
- Significance of the audit evidence obtained
- Nature and extent of exceptions identified
- Need to document a conclusion or the basis for a conclusion not readily determinable from the documentation of the work performed or audit evidence obtained
- Audit methodology and tools used
- Extent of judgment involved in performing the work and evaluating the results

For each audit procedure performed, the auditor should document the following:

- The identifying characteristics of the specific items or matters tested
- Who performed the audit work and the date work was completed
- Who reviewed the audit work along with the date and extent of such review

Best practices for audit documentation

The November 2017 issue of the *Journal of Accountancy* highlights the following four best practices for effective audit documentation.

1. Take a smart approach to planning by mapping the audit in a memo to lay out the biggest risks, strategies to mitigate each risk, and references to where and how work is to be performed. Reference the audit plan frequently and revise the memo as the audit progresses and new risks are identified.
2. Embrace standardization across your organization and let go of immaterial personal preferences that may lead to inconsistencies and inefficiencies. Additionally, document with intent and do not allow unnecessary client documentation to clutter the client file.
3. Document while performing audit procedures, instead of waiting to catch up on documentation later. This approach will ultimately save time and ensure high quality documentation. Additionally, issuing the audit report timely helps limit the auditor's responsibility for subsequent events procedures.
4. Document with the future in mind. Ensure that this year's documentation will provide next year's audit team with a solid foundation. This will help eliminate future rework and inefficiencies.

Knowledge check

9. Final assembly of the audit documentation in an audit file should be completed no later than when?

   a. 45 days following the audit report date.
   b. 60 days following the audit report date.
   c. 45 days following the report release date.
   d. 60 days following the report release date.

Improper risk assessment

The goal of identifying, assessing, and responding to risks of material misstatement is at the heart of every audit and drives every audit procedure, and yet, an AICPA Peer Review Program study found that more than 1 in 10 firms are not properly assessing risk or linking their assessments to their audit procedures. In fact, more than 10 years after the SAS Nos. 104–111 provided a new road map for executing the audit, many auditors still believe they can perform a quality audit without properly assessing their client's risks. In reality, without assess their clients' risks, an auditor will have no basis for designing a quality audit plan that addresses those risks. As a result, auditors will have no way of knowing whether their procedures and substantive testing actually reduce audit risk to an appropriately low level.

Non-conformity related to misconceived notions about the importance of risk assessment is particularly prevalent in small- to medium-sized entities and is leading to violations of professional standards.

The most common areas of noncompliance found in the AICPA Peer Review Program study were:

- 40% of identified issues related to failure to gain an understanding of internal control when identifying the client's risks.
- 14% of issues related to incomplete or nonexistent risk assessment.
- 24% of issues related to auditors not linking their risk assessment to their response
- 13% of issues related to auditors assessing control risk as less than high without appropriate tests of controls.

The risk assessment process is important for every audit, regardless of the size or industry in which the client operates. An effective risk assessment requires an auditor to first obtain an understanding of the client and its environment. This includes gaining knowledge of internal control relevant to the audit, evaluating the design of those controls, and assessing whether the controls have been implemented. Once this understanding of the client is established, audit procedures can be designed that are clearly linked and responsive to the risks identified. This is sometimes referred to as a "top-down" approach because it starts with a broader understanding of the client, not at the procedure level. Although the AICPA does not require an auditor to test the operating effectiveness of an internal control, procedures around design and implementation must be performed.

Audit risk model

Audit risk is the risk that the firm will issue the wrong audit opinion when the financial statements are materially misstated. This includes inherent risk (the risk of material misstatement assuming there are no related controls); control risk (the risk that the client's controls will not prevent or detect a material misstatement); and detection risk (the risk that the auditor will not detect a material misstatement). Inherent and control risk combine to form risk of material misstatement, or RMM.

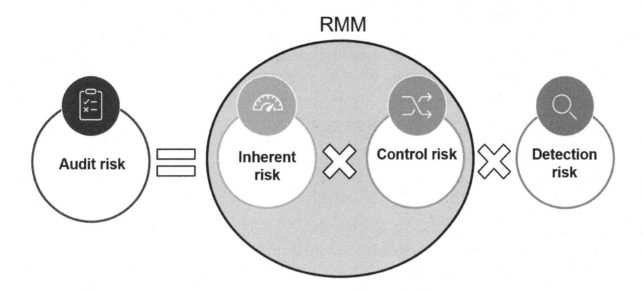

The risk of material misstatement is the risk that the financial statements are materially misstated prior to the audit. This consists of two components, inherent risk and control risk, which are defined in AU-C section 200.

- Inherent risk: The susceptibility of an assertion about a class of transaction, account balance, or disclosure to a misstatement that could be material, either individually or when aggregated with other misstatements, before consideration of any related controls.
- Control risk: The risk that a misstatement that could occur in an assertion about a class of transaction, account balance, or disclosure and that could be material, either individually or when aggregated with other misstatements, will not be prevented, or detected and corrected, on a timely basis by the entity's internal control.

In order to express an opinion with a reasonable level of assurance, an auditor must reduce audit risk to an acceptably low level. The only way for the auditor to control audit risk is to drive detection risk (the risk that audit procedures will not detect misstatement) to a low level. As implied in the audit risk model, the higher the risks of material misstatement, the more work needs to be done to reduce detection risk.

Paragraph .03 of AU-C section 315 says that risk assessment provides "a basis for designing and implementing responses to the assessed risks of material misstatement." In other words, to perform an audit in accordance with professional standards, the auditor should

- first, gain an understanding of the client and its internal controls to identify the client's risks of material misstatement, then
- assess the identified risks; and
- finally, design procedures that respond to those risks.

If auditors do not assess their clients' risks, they will have no basis for designing audit plans with procedures that respond to those risks. Regardless of the amount and type of substantive testing they perform, the auditors will have no way of knowing whether their procedures reduced audit risk to an appropriately low level. As such, a failure to comply with AU-C section 315 represents a failure to obtain sufficient appropriate audit evidence to support the opinion.

Significant risks are defined in AU-C section 315 as "an identified and assessed risk of material misstatement that, in the auditor's professional judgment, requires special audit consideration." Significant risks often relate to significant nonroutine transactions and matters that require significant judgment. Routine noncomplex transactions that are subject to systematic processing are less likely to give rise to significant risks.

In exercising professional judgment about which risks are significant risks, an auditor should consider the following:

- Whether the risk is a risk of fraud
- Whether the risk is related to recent significant economic, accounting, or other developments and, therefore, requires specific attention
- The complexity of transactions
- Whether the risk involves significant transactions with related parties
- The degree of subjectivity in the measurement of financial information related to the risk, especially those measurements involving a wide range of measurement uncertainty
- Whether the risk involves significant transactions that are outside the normal course of business for the entity or that otherwise appear to be unusual
  - Such non-routine transactions are often less likely to be subject to routine controls. However, management may have other responses intended to deal with such risks.

Assertions are representations by management, explicit or otherwise, that are embodied in the financial statements as used by the auditor to consider the different types of potential misstatements that may occur. A **relevant assertion is then a** financial statement assertion that has a **reasonable possibility** of containing a misstatement or misstatements that would cause the financial statements to be materially misstated. The determination of whether an assertion is a relevant assertion is made without regard to the effect of internal controls.

Examples of assertions include: occurrence, existence, completeness, cutoff, classification, accuracy, valuation and allocation, understandability, and rights and obligations.

Audit procedures are designed to respond to assertion-level risks, so the risks should be assessed at the following:

- The relevant assertion-level. This means an auditor should assess risk for assertions that have a reasonable possibility of material misstatement. It does not, however, mean every assertion for every account.
- The financial statement-level. This means an auditor should assess risks which are pervasive to the financials and which would affect numerous assertions, such as high turnover of key roles in the accounting department. Ultimately, an auditor will aim to identify the specific assertions that financial statement level risks will impact.

Common audit deficiencies found by the AICPA include assessing risk at the account level in lieu of the assertion level.

As a reminder, performing risk assessment procedures such as identifying and assessing risk, do not reduce control risk. The only way to reduce control risk is to test the operating effectiveness of the controls. The AICPA does not require the testing of controls except when the auditor plans to rely on the controls and reduce control risk.

Linkage is key

It was found that many auditors, particularly those serving smaller clients, appear to be documenting risk assessments in accordance with AU-C section 315. However, they would then proceed to perform the audit with little regard to the results of that assessment (such as using a standard set of procedures or following the same pattern as last year's audit). By failing to link their audit procedures to the completed risk assessment they are not taking credit for the work they've done by focusing their procedures on addressing the client's risks. Instead they are often performing significant substantive procedures on every audit area regardless of risk. This leads to inefficiency and over-auditing in some areas and can lead to noncompliance in other areas if the auditor did not address the risks properly.

What if the client has no controls?

A common misconception is the belief that a client can have no controls. Conversely, even the smallest of reporting entities has some controls, although they may be weak or high-level. Because a control is any policy or procedure used by a reporting entity to prevent, or detect and correct, a misstatement, claiming that a reporting entity has no controls would suggest that an entity has no ability to prevent, or detect and correct, any type of misstatement. Such a suggestion would call into question the auditor's ability to express an opinion with a reasonable level of assurance regardless of how many procedures they perform.

Even the smallest of reporting entities have some controls, like the following:

- Monitoring by business owners or management
- Computer login credentials
- Communications from management to employees about the importance of doing things right

More common than a complete lack of controls is incomplete documentation of controls. At smaller nonpublic entities, there may be certain controls that have been put in place but have not been formally documented. Even without proper client documentation, an auditor may test a control as part of an audit. In this case, it may also be appropriate to issue a management recommendation that the client have a formal documentation process for any controls they have established and placed in operation.

As a reminder, the five components of internal control are the following:

- Control environment
- Entity's risk assessment process
- Information system, including the related business processes relevant to financial reporting, and communication
- Control activities employed by the organization
- Monitoring of controls

Improper use of third-party practice aids

Standardized, third-party practice aids can be valuable tools that provide auditors with useful insights when planning and conducting an audit. However, such tools are not intended to be used in place of a risk assessment. Even if auditors use standardized practice aids, they are still required to perform a risk assessment and show the linkage between that assessment and their procedures. Auditors are never to assume that recommended procedures in standardized practice aids will address a particular client's specific risks. Tailoring audit programs from third party practice aids ensures that risks have been properly addressed.

Even clients of similar size in the same industry will not have the exact same risks and thus will not require the exact same audit responses. As noted earlier, a strong understanding of a client and its environment, policies, and controls is necessary to design procedures that specifically address their unique significant risks.

Tips for addressing risk in audit engagements:

- Obtain a strong understanding of the client and its environment, including the system of internal control.
- Identify the client's risks, including any significant risks.
- Document the linkage between the risk assessment and the procedures on the audit programs.
- Design and perform procedures that specifically address any significant risks.
- Revisit the risk assessment and audit plan throughout the engagement.
- Utilize free tools available at https://www.aicpa.org/content/aicpa/eaq/aicpa-risk-assessment-resources.html to document the risk assessment, train staff, or help perform an effective internal inspection.

When documenting the audit, an auditor should include the following:

- Overall responses to address the assessed risks of material misstatement at the financial statement level and the nature, timing, and extent of the further audit procedures performed
- Linkage of those procedures with the assessed risks at the relevant assertion level
- Results of the audit procedures, including the conclusions when such conclusions are not otherwise clear

The AICPA does not have required terminology for assessing risk. Some practice aids use a numbering system, others use high, moderate and low. The standards makes no reference to proper terminology. As always, the form and extent of audit documentation is a matter of professional judgment. It is influenced by the nature, size, and complexity of the entity, the internal control environment, availability of information from the entity, and the audit methodology and technology used by the auditor.

Impact on peer review

The Peer Review Board approved a new section to the AICPA Peer Review Program Manual, PRP section 3100, *Evaluation of Noncompliance with the Risk Assessment Standards*, effective for reviews commencing on or after October 1, 2018 through reviews commencing on or before September 30, 2021.[4]

---

[4] The AICPA Peer Review Manual can be found at https://www.aicpa.org/interestareas/peerreview/resources/peerreviewprogrammanual.html, and PRP section 3100 may be found at https://www.aicpa.org/content/dam/aicpa/research/standards/peerreview/downloadabledocuments/guidance.pdf.

If a peer reviewer finds noncompliance with the risk assessment standards, the engagement should be deemed non-conforming.

If the noncompliance is not considered isolated, they should issue the following:

- A finding if no deficiencies or significant deficiencies related to other engagement performance issues are noted, even if all the engagements reviewed are nonconforming solely due to noncompliance with the risk assessment standards.
- A deficiency or significant deficiency if deficiencies and significant deficiencies related to other omitted audit procedures exist.
- A finding if there are deficiencies or significant deficiencies related to elements of a firm's system of quality control that did not result in omitted audit procedures (for example, monitoring or tone at the top).

Non-compliance noted	Isolated or Systemic	Conclusion
Failure to comply with the Risk Assessment Standards	Isolated	MFC
Failure to comply with the Risk Assessment Standards	Systemic	FFC and Implementation Plan
Failure to comply with the Risk Assessment Standards and other deficiencies or significant deficiencies exist	Systemic	Deficiency or Significant Deficiency with Corrective Action

Changes are currently being made to Peer Review Integrated Management Application (PRIMA) to allow peer reviewers to indicate the number of non-conforming engagements due to noncompliance with the risk assessment standards. This will provide a mechanism for the AICPA to track the effectiveness of the initiative. These changes are expected to be implemented in early 2019.

Other resources available to auditors and peer reviewers include the Internal Inspection Practice Aid *Addressing Noncompliance with AU-C 315 and 330* at https://www.aicpa.org/content/dam/aicpa/interestareas/peerreview/eaq/eaq-risk-internal-inspection-aid.pdf.

Appendix 1A

DOCUMENTATION CASE STUDY

For each example in part 1 and part 2, indicate whether the documentation standard has been met. If not, what attributes of adequate documentation are missing?

Part 1

Client has one note receivable, and the note balance is material to the financial statements.

Auditor tested the note for existence, rights, and valuation.

No significant findings or issues were noted.

No significant judgments were made.

Example 1

Audit program step	Preparer signoff and date	Reviewer signoff and date
Obtain and review note(s) receivable. Test existence, rights and valuation assertions.	CRM 3/30/X7	BAM 4/2/X7

1. Has the auditor documented the nature and extent of the procedures, including the identifying characteristics of the items tested?
2. Has the auditor documented the timing of the procedures?
3. Has the auditor documented the results of the procedures?

Example 2

Audit program step	Preparer signoff and date	Reviewer signoff and date
Obtain and review note(s) receivable. Test existence, rights and valuation assertions.	CRM 3/30/X7	BAM 4/2/X7

CRM Note: Controller provided audit team with note issued 11/17/20X6. Reviewed note, verifying existence and that the entity is the holder of the note. Received letter from the borrower (see working paper B200) confirming the face amount of $112,000 was outstanding at fiscal year-end and matures on 5/31/X7. Tied face amount back to TB.

1. Has the auditor documented the nature and extent of the procedures, including the identifying characteristics of the items tested?
2. Has the auditor documented the timing of the procedures?
3. Has the auditor documented the results of the procedures?

Part 2

Client has numerous notes receivable, and the total balance is material to the financial statements.

Auditor has concluded (and documented, as part of planning) that notes with balances over $70,000 will be subject to testing. Auditor tested certain notes for existence, rights, and valuation.

No significant findings or issues were noted.

No significant judgments were made.

Example 3

Audit program step	Preparer signoff and date	Reviewer signoff and date
Obtain and review note(s) receivable. Test existence, rights and valuation assertions.	CRM 3/30/X7	BAM 4/2/X7
CRM Note: Selected a sample of notes for testing. Notes were provided by controller. Reviewed notes, testing for existence, rights and valuation. No exceptions noted.		

1. Has the auditor documented the nature and extent of the procedures, including the identifying characteristics of the items tested?
2. Has the auditor documented the timing of the procedures?
3. Has the auditor documented the results of the procedures?

Example 4

Client Name	Example Company 2	Working Paper #	EX-2
Working Paper Title	Short-Term Notes Receivable	Preparer	CRM
Balance Sheet Date	12/31/20x6	Date Completed	3/30/X7
Prepared By Client?	No	Reviewer	BAM
		Date Reviewed	4/2/X7

Objective: To verify that the notes receivable appearing on the balance sheet exist, Example Company 2 has rights to them, and their valuation is appropriate.

Customer's Name	Issue Date	Maturity Date	Face Amount	
Customer A	11/17/20x6	5/19/20x7	112,000.00	T, C, Ⓐ
Customer B	9/15/20x6	6/30/20x7	330,000.00	T, C, Ⓐ
Customer C	9/1/20x6	4/5/20x7	72,000.00	T, C, Ⓐ
Customer D	7/24/20x6	6/18/20x7	91,000.00	T, C, Ⓐ
			605,000.00	

Tickmark Legend

T Traced face amount, issue and maturity dates to note

C Agreed to confirmation

Ⓐ Agreed to client's list of notes receivable at working paper EX-2a, which ties to Trial Balance

1. Has the auditor documented the nature and extent of the procedures, including the identifying characteristics of the items tested?
2. Has the auditor documented the timing of the procedures?
3. Has the auditor documented the results of the procedures?

Appendix 1B

EXAMPLE AUDITOR'S REPORT AND CASE STUDY

Independent Auditor's Report

[Appropriate Addressee]

Report on the Audit of the Financial Statements[1]

Opinion

We have audited the financial statements of XYZ Not-for-Profit Organization, which comprise the statement of financial position as of September 30, 20X1, and the related statements of activities and cash flows for the year then ended, and the related notes to the financial statements.

In our opinion, the accompanying financial statements present fairly, in all material respects, the financial position of XYZ Not-for-Profit Organization as of September 30, 20X1, and the results of its operations and its cash flows for the year then ended in accordance with accounting principles generally accepted in the United States of America.

Basis for Opinion

We conducted our audits in accordance with auditing standards generally accepted in the United States of America (GAAS). Our responsibilities under those standards are further described in the Auditor's Responsibilities for the Audit of the Financial Statements section of our report. We are required to be independent of XYZ Not-for-Profit Organization and to meet our other ethical responsibilities, in accordance with the relevant ethical requirements relating to our audits. We believe that the audit evidence we have obtained is sufficient and appropriate to provide a basis for our audit opinion.

Key Audit Matters

[This section of the auditor's report is included only if the auditor is engaged to communicate key audit matters.]

Key audit matters are those matters that were communicated with those charged with governance and, in our professional judgment, were of most significance in our audit of the financial statements of the current period. These matters were addressed in the context of our audit of the financial statements as a whole, and in forming our opinion thereon, and we do not provide a separate opinion on these matters.

[*Description of each key audit matter in accordance with section* 701, Communicating Key Audit Matters in the Independent Auditor's Report]

Responsibilities of Management for the Financial Statements

Management is responsible for the preparation and fair presentation of the financial statements in accordance with accounting principles generally accepted in the United States of America, and for the design, implementation, and maintenance of internal control relevant to the preparation and fair presentation of financial statements that are free from material misstatement, whether due to fraud or error.

---

[1] The subtitle "Report on the Audit of the Financial Statements" is unnecessary in circumstances in which the second subtitle, "Report on Other Legal and Regulatory Requirements," is not applicable.

In preparing the financial statements, management is required to evaluate whether there are conditions or events, considered in the aggregate, that raise substantial doubt about the Company's ability to continue as a going concern for [*insert the time period set by the applicable financial reporting framework, which for FASB-reporting entities is one year after the date that the financial statements are issued (or within one year after the date that the financial statements are available to be issued, when applicable)*].

Auditor's Responsibilities for the Audit of the Financial Statements

Our objectives are to obtain reasonable assurance about whether the financial statements as a whole are free from material misstatement, whether due to fraud or error, and to issue an auditor's report that includes our opinion. Reasonable assurance is a high level of assurance but is not absolute assurance and therefore is not a guarantee that an audit conducted in accordance with GAAS will always detect a material misstatement when it exists. The risk of not detecting a material misstatement resulting from fraud is higher than for one resulting from error, as fraud may involve collusion, forgery, intentional omissions, misrepresentations, or the override of internal control. Misstatements are considered material if there is a substantial likelihood that, individually or in the aggregate, they would influence the judgment made by a reasonable user based on the financial statements.

In performing an audit in accordance with GAAS, we:

- Exercise professional judgment and maintain professional skepticism throughout the audit.
- Identify and assess the risks of material misstatement of the financial statements, whether due to fraud or error, and design and perform audit procedures responsive to those risks. Such procedures include examining, on a test basis, evidence regarding the amounts and disclosures in the financial statements.
- Obtain an understanding of internal control relevant to the audit in order to design audit procedures that are appropriate in the circumstances, but not for the purpose of expressing an opinion on the effectiveness of the XYZ Not-for-Profit Organization's internal control. Accordingly, no such opinion is expressed.[2]
- Evaluate the appropriateness of accounting policies used and the reasonableness of significant accounting estimates made by management, as well as evaluate the overall presentation of the financial statements.
- Conclude whether, in our judgment, there are conditions or events, considered in the aggregate, that raise substantial doubt about XYZ Not-for-Profit Organization's ability to continue as a going concern for a reasonable period of time.

We are required to communicate with those charged with governance regarding, among other matters, the planned scope and timing of the audit, significant audit findings, and certain internal control related matters that we identified during the audit.

Other Information [or another title, if appropriate, such as "Information Other Than the Financial Statements and Auditor's Report Thereon"]

---

[2] In circumstances in which the auditor also has responsibility to express an opinion on the effectiveness of internal control in conjunction with the audit of the financial statements, omit the following: "but not for the purpose of expressing an opinion on the effectiveness of XYZ Not-for-Profit Organization's internal control. Accordingly, no such opinion is expressed."

[Reporting in accordance with the reporting requirements in AU-C section 720, The Auditor's Responsibilities Relating to Other Information Included in Annual Reports (refer to illustrations in the exhibit of AU-C section 720)][3]

Report on Other Legal and Regulatory Requirements

[The form and content of this section of the auditor's report would vary depending on the nature of the auditor's other reporting responsibilities.]

[Signature of the auditor's firm]

[City and state where the auditor's report is issued]

[Date of the auditor's report]

Case Study Part 1

Draw a line to the corresponding section header for each statement below:

We believe that the audit evidence we have obtained is sufficient and appropriate to provide a basis for our audit opinion.	Management's responsibility
Misstatements are considered material if there is a substantial likelihood that, individually or in the aggregate, they would influence the judgment made by a reasonable user based on the financial statements.	
Key audit matters are those matters that were communicated with those charged with governance and, in our professional judgment, were of most significance in our audit of the financial statements of the current period.	Key Audit Matters
In our opinion, the accompanying financial statements present fairly, in all material respects, the financial position of NFP Entity as of December 31, 20X1 and 20X0, and the results of its operations and its cash flows for the years then ended in accordance with accounting principles generally accepted in the United States of America.	

---

[3] Paragraph .24 of SAS No. 137, The Auditor's Responsibilities Relating to Other Information Included in Annual Reports, describes the separate section of the auditor's report that is required if other information, whether financial or nonfinancial, is included in an entity's annual report, as defined. SAS No. 137 is effective for audits of financial statements for periods ending on or after December 15, 2020. Early implementation is not permitted. This appendix has not been updated for SAS No. 137. Readers are also encouraged to consult the full text of the SAS at https://www.aicpa.org/interestareas/frc/auditattest/auditing-standards-information-and-resources.html.

Reasonable assurance is a high level of assurance but is not absolute assurance and therefore is not a guarantee that an audit conducted in accordance with GAAS will always detect a material misstatement when it exists.	Auditor's Responsibility
We are required to be independent of ABC Company and to meet our other ethical responsibilities, in accordance with the relevant ethical requirements relating to our audits.	Opinion
We have audited the financial statements of NFP Entity, which comprise the balance sheets as of December 31, 20X1 and 20X0, and the related statements of income, changes in stockholders' equity, and cash flows for the years then ended, and the related notes to the financial statements.	
These matters were addressed in the context of our audit of the financial statements as a whole, and in forming our opinion thereon, and we do not provide a separate opinion on these matters. Our objectives are to obtain reasonable assurance about whether the financial statements as a whole are free from material misstatement, whether due to fraud or error, and to issue an auditor's report that includes our opinion.	Basis for Opinion
The risk of not detecting a material misstatement resulting from fraud is higher than for one resulting from error, as fraud may involve collusion, forgery, intentional omissions, misrepresentations, or the override of internal control.	
We conducted our audits in accordance with auditing standards generally accepted in the United States of America (GAAS).	

Case Study Part 2

Based on the updated report in SAS 134, fill in the blank with the word(s) that properly completes the sentence:

Exercise professional _____ and maintain professional skepticism throughout the audit.

Identify and _____ the risks of material misstatement of the financial statements, whether due to fraud or _____, and design and perform audit procedures responsive to those risks.

Obtain an _____ of internal control relevant to the audit in order to design audit procedures that are appropriate in the circumstances, but not for the purpose of expressing an opinion on the effectiveness of the ABC Company's internal control.

Evaluate the _____ of accounting policies used and the reasonableness of significant accounting estimates made by management, as well as evaluate the overall _____ of the financial statements.

Conclude whether, in our judgment, there are conditions or events, considered in the _____, that raise substantial doubt about ABC Company's ability to continue as a going concern for a _____ period of time.

In our opinion, the accompanying financial statements present fairly, in all _____ respects, the financial position of NFP Entity as of December 31, 20X1 and 20X0, and the results of its operations and its cash flows for the years then ended in accordance with accounting principles generally accepted in the United States of America.

Key audit matters are those matters that were communicated with those charged with governance and, in our professional judgment, were of most _____ in our audit of the financial statements of the current period.

Management is responsible for the _____ and fair presentation of the financial statements in accordance with accounting principles generally accepted in the United States of America, and for the design, implementation, and _____ of internal control relevant to the preparation and fair presentation of financial statements that are free from material misstatement, whether due to _____ or _____.

In preparing the financial statements, _____ is required to evaluate whether there are conditions or events, considered in the aggregate, that raise substantial doubt about the Company's ability to continue as a going concern for [insert the time period set by the applicable financial reporting framework].

Our _____ are to obtain _____ assurance about whether the financial statements as a whole are free from material misstatement, whether due to fraud or error, and to issue an auditor's report that includes our _____.

_____ assurance is a _____ level of assurance but is not _____ assurance and therefore is not a guarantee that an audit conducted in accordance with GAAS will _____ detect a material misstatement when it exists.

The risk of not detecting a material misstatement resulting from _____ is higher than for one resulting from _____, as fraud may involve collusion, forgery, intentional omissions, misrepresentations, or the override of internal control.

Appendix 1C

NOT-FOR-PROFIT ACCOUNTING
AND AUDIT COMPETENCY RESOURCE

Not-for-profit member section

In May 2015, the AICPA launched a new membership section for CPAs in public practice as well as those who work with or for a not-for-profit. The AICPA's Not-for-Profit Section (NFP section) provides support and resources in the areas of audit, financial accounting, and tax for members and other finance professionals. Those who have management or governance responsibilities, including those who serve as board members or as volunteers, are eligible to join the AICPA as a non-CPA associate. AICPA members, including, associates and non-CPA associates are eligible to join the NFP Section.

Benefits for NFP section members include the following:

- Timely communications covering breaking news. E-alerts and interactive webcasts will inform members when standard setters and regulatory agencies issue new guidance.
- Tools and resources. There is a wide-range of information including articles and tools that provide a deeper dive into topics such as risk management, communicating with audit committees, allocation of functional expenses, and Form 990 red flags.
- Sample financial statements and note disclosures.
- Board governance and accounting policy examples.
- Tools including a Form 990 worksheet, internal control checklists, example management letter comments, and reference charts.
- CPE-eligible courses.

NFP certificate programs

The AICPA offers two certificate programs for not-for-profit professionals. These programs are available to anyone with an interest in learning more about financial management of NFPs.

Not-For-Profit Certificate I

The Not-for-Profit (NFP) Certificate I program is specially designed to help accountants and others build the knowledge needed to gain a basic understanding of these entities by providing a foundation in not-for-profit accounting, tax compliance, governance and assurance. The program provides 24 courses on demand, which total 40 hours of CPE delivered in three topical tracks.

Participants learn about GAAP reporting standards that apply to NFPs, including financial statement presentation and disclosure requirements, state and federal filing requirements for tax-exempt organizations, best practices in board governance, financial oversight, internal controls, fraud, and other risks, and audit planning considerations.

Not-for-Profit Certificate II

A more advanced version, Not-For-Profit Certificate II, provides 30 hours of CPE through 17 courses that build on the core principles presented in the first program. There is no requirement to complete Certificate I to take Certificate II. The program is offered online using video presented by leading NFP industry experts. Topics include how to prepare financial statements, how to complete IRS Form 990, how to build complex budgets, how to perform risk assessments, how to guide the strategic planning process, and how to work with an NFP's governing board. Learning exercises, targeted case studies, and detail-rich interpretations are interspersed throughout the video presentations.

Chapter 2

FASB Activities

Learning objectives

- Identify FASB's recently issued Accounting Standards Updates (ASUs) affecting not-for-profit (NFP) entities.

- Determine the impact of revenue recognition standards on NFP entities.

FASB resource groups

Not-for-profit Advisory Committee

Several years ago, FASB added a staff member dedicated to advising the board and other staff on issues affecting NFP entities and communicating with members in the NFP sector. To provide additional guidance to the board, FASB established the Not-for-Profit Advisory Committee (NAC) in October 2009.

The NAC works closely with FASB in an advisory capacity to ensure that the perspectives from the NFP sector are effectively communicated to FASB on a timely basis. Other responsibilities of the NAC are as follows:

- To provide focused input and feedback relating to
    - the need for and relative priority of proposed FASB projects;
    - conceptual and practical implications of proposals under development in active projects; and
    - practice issues including implementation issues arising from new standards, potential areas for improvement pertinent to the NFP sector, and longer-term issues important to the NFP sector.

- To assist FASB and its staff with communication and outreach activities to the NFP sector on
  - recent standards and other existing guidance;
  - current and proposed projects; and
  - longer-term issues.
- Advise on other matters for which FASB may seek guidance

The NAC comprises 15 to 20 members who demonstrate the following:

- A keen interest in and knowledge of financial accounting and reporting matters
- Experience working within the NFP sector
- A commitment to improving financial reporting for users of financial statements
- The ability to provide input on a wide variety of financial reporting matters

Not-for-Profit Resource Group

In addition to the NAC, FASB has Not-for-Profit Resource Group (NRG) whose members primarily serve as a resource to the NAC. Periodically, all members of the NRG or particular types of members (for example preparers, auditors, creditors, donors and grantors, and so on) are surveyed on matters of interest to the NAC.

Revenue recognition and leases

ASU No. 2014-09, *Revenue from Contracts with Customers (Topic 606), as amended*[1]

Why was this ASU issued?

The objective of ASU No. 2014-09, as amended, is to address a number of concerns regarding the complexity and lack of consistency surrounding the accounting for revenue transactions. In addition, ASU No. 2014-09, as amended, provides a framework for revenue recognition and eliminates the transaction and industry-specific revenue recognition guidance. The intent is to avoid inconsistencies of accounting treatment across different geographies and industries.

Who is affected by this update?

This ASU, as amended, affects any entity that either enters into contracts

- with customers to transfer goods or services; and
- for the transfer of nonfinancial assets unless those contracts are within the scope of other standards (for example, lease or insurance contracts).

NFP entities that classify government and other grants as exchange transactions will need to account for those agreements using the guidance in ASU No. 2014-09, as amended.

What are the main provisions of this ASU?

The core principle of the revised revenue recognition standard is that an entity should recognize revenue to depict the transfer of goods or services to customers in an amount that reflects the consideration to which the entity expects to be entitled in exchange for those good or services. ASU No. 2014-09 focuses on contracts with customers. Because donors are not customers, contributions are not within the scope of this standard.

ASU No. 2014-09, as amended, states that an entity should follow these five steps in recognizing revenue from contracts with customers:

1. Identify the contract(s) with a customer.
2. Identify the performance obligations in the contract.
3. Determine the transaction price.

---

[1] The effective date of this ASU was amended upon issuance of ASU No. 2015-14, *Revenue from Contracts with Customers (Topic 606): Deferral of the Effective Date.*

4. Allocate the transaction price to the performance obligations in the contract.
5. Recognize revenue when (or as) the entity satisfies a performance obligation.

Key point
Under ASU No. 2014-09, as amended, revenue is recognized when an entity satisfies a performance obligation by transferring a promised good or service to a customer (which is when the customer obtains control of that good or service).

Understanding the five-step process

Step 1: Identify the contract(s) with a customer

ASU No. 2014-09, as amended, defines a *contract* as "an agreement between two or more parties that creates enforceable rights and obligations." This update affects contracts with a customer that meets the following criteria:

- Approval (in writing, orally, or in accordance with other customary business practices) and commitment of the parties is in place
- Rights of the parties are identified
- Payment terms are identified
- Contract has commercial substance
- It is probable that the entity will collect the consideration to which it will be entitled in exchange for the goods or services that will be transferred to the customer

A contract does not exist if each party to the contract has the unilateral enforceable right to terminate a wholly unperformed contract without compensating the other party (parties).

Step 2: Identify the performance obligations in the contract

A *performance obligation* is defined by FASB as a promise in a contract with a customer to transfer a good or service to the customer.

At contract inception, an entity should assess the goods or services promised in a contract with a customer and should identify as a performance obligation (possibly multiple performance obligations) each promise to transfer to the customer either

- a good or service (or bundle of goods or services) that is distinct, or
- a series of distinct goods or services that are substantially the same and that have the same pattern of transfer to the customer.

A good or service that is not distinct should be combined with other promised goods or services until the entity identifies a bundle of goods or services that is distinct. In some cases, that would result in the entity accounting for all the goods or services promised in a contract as a single performance obligation.

Step 3: Determine the transaction price

The transaction price is the amount of consideration (fixed or variable) the entity expects to receive in exchange for transferring promised goods or services to a customer, excluding amounts collected on behalf of third parties. To determine the transaction price, an entity should consider the effects of

- variable consideration,
- constraining estimates of variable consideration,
- the existence of a significant financing component,
- noncash considerations, and
- consideration payable to the customer.

If the consideration promised in a contract includes a variable amount, then an entity should estimate the amount of consideration to which the entity will be entitled in exchange for transferring the promised goods or services to a customer. An entity would then include in the transaction price some or all of an amount of variable consideration only to the extent that it is probable that a significant reversal in the amount of cumulative revenue recognized will not occur when the uncertainty associated with the variable consideration is subsequently resolved.

An entity should consider the terms of the contract and its customary business practices to determine the transaction price.

Step 4: Allocate the transaction price to the performance obligations in the contract

The transaction price is allocated to separate performance obligations in proportion to the stand-alone selling price of the promised goods or services. If a stand-alone selling price is not directly observable, then an entity should estimate it. Reallocation of the transaction price for changes in the stand-alone selling price is not permitted. When estimating the stand-alone selling price, entities can use various methods including the adjusted market assessment approach, expected cost plus a margin approach, and residual approach (only if the selling price is highly variable and uncertain).

ASU No. 2014-09, as amended, specifies when an entity should allocate any discount or variable consideration relating to one performance obligation to that (or some other) performance obligation rather than to all the performance obligations in the contract.

Step 5: Recognize revenue when (or as) the entity satisfies a performance obligation

The amount of revenue recognized when transferring the promised good or service to a customer is equal to the amount allocated to the satisfied performance obligation, which may be satisfied at a point in time (goods) or over time (services).

Under ASU No. 2014-09, entities may recognize revenue over time only if one of the following criteria is met:

- The customer simultaneously receives and consumes the benefits provided by the entity's performance as the entity performs.
- The entity's performance creates or enhances an asset (that is, work in process) that the customer controls as the asset is created or enhanced.
- The entity's performance does not create an asset with an alternative use to the entity, and the entity has an enforceable right to payment for performance completed to date.

Key point
In the context of ASU No. 2014-09, as amended, control of an asset refers to the ability to direct the use of, and obtain substantially all the remaining benefits from, the asset. Control also includes the ability to prevent other entities from directing the use of, and obtaining the benefits from, an asset.

When performance obligations are satisfied over time, the entity should select an appropriate method for measuring its progress toward complete satisfaction of that performance obligation. ASU No. 2014-09, as amended, discusses methods of measuring progress including input and output methods, and how to determine which method is appropriate.

Additional guidance under this ASU

ASU No. 2014-09 also addresses the following areas:

- Accounting for incremental costs of obtaining a contract, as well as costs incurred to fulfill a contract
- Licenses
- Warranties

Lastly, ASU No. 2014-09, as amended, enhances disclosure requirements to include more information about specific revenue contracts entered into by the entity, including qualitative and quantitative information about contracts with customers, significant judgments and changes in those judgments, and assets recognized from the costs to obtain or fulfill a contract.

A thorough discussion of the full text of ASU No. 2014-09, as amended, is beyond the scope of this chapter and this course. Readers are strongly encouraged to read the full update, which is available at www.fasb.org.

When is this ASU effective?

For nonpublic entities, including NFP entities without conduit debt, this ASU, as amended, is effective for annual reporting periods beginning after December 15, 2018, and interim periods within annual periods beginning after December 15, 2019. Nonpublic business entities and other entities may elect to adopt the standard earlier but no earlier than the annual periods beginning after December 15, 2016.

Implementation issues

Generally, to successfully implement the requirements of this standard, entities first need to evaluate how the standard affects the entity overall. This should include consideration of the effects not only on the financial statements but other information systems, processes, compensation, and other contractual commitments, and tax planning strategies. All entities affected by this ASU need to develop an implementation plan. At a minimum, an implementation plan will need to include

- key actions for implementation,
- time estimated for each implementation action, and
- a mechanism to track the progress and timing of the implementation plan.

This ASU, as amended, is likely to affect NFP entities that account for government and other grants or membership dues in whole or in part as exchange transactions.

Many NFP entities enter into multiple-year grants or membership contracts, or both. Any grant agreements or membership contracts signed prior to the effective date of ASU No. 2014-09, as amended, will require retrospective restatement upon the deferred effective date of ASU No. 2014-09. This could have significant negative consequences if revenue has been recognized prior to transition that does not meet the requirements for recognition under ASU No. 2014-09, as amended. If performance obligations are not clearly delineated in the grant agreement or membership contract, revenue is not recognized until the contract terminates.

Knowledge check

1. Which is **not** in the scope of FASB's revenue recognition standard, as amended?

    a. Grants that are determined to be exchange transactions.
    b. Sales from an NFP store.
    c. Donor contributions.
    d. Sponsorships that are part exchange and part contribution.

2. In order to be recognized separately, performance obligations must be

    a. Discrete.
    b. Distinct.
    c. Divergent.
    d. Disparate.

ASU No. 2018-08, *Not-for-Profit Entities (Topic 958): Clarifying the Scope and the Accounting Guidance for Contributions Received and Contributions Made*

Why was this ASU issued?

The NAC as well as the AICPA's NFP Expert Panel have raised concerns with the difficulty in practice among NFPs with characterizing grants and similar contracts with government agencies as either exchange transactions (reciprocal) or contributions (nonreciprocal). This has been a longstanding issue for NFPs. However, with the impending implementation of the revenue recognition standard, it has become more important for NFPs to get the classification correct. ASU No. 2014-09 applies to exchange transactions, not contributions. Despite the degree of existing guidance, there is significant diversity in practice on the conclusions being reached in these scenarios. In some instances, similar grants are accounted for as contributions (nonreciprocal transactions, generally conditional) by some NFPs and as exchange transactions (reciprocal transactions) by other NFPs.

What are the main provisions of this ASU?

The ASU clarifies when the resource provider is receiving commensurate value. FASB indicated that a *resource provider* is not synonymous with *the general public* and *indirect benefit received by the public as a result of the assets transferred* is not equivalent to *commensurate value received by the resource provider*. In addition, execution of a resource provider's mission or the positive sentiment from acting as a donor does not constitute commensurate value received by a resource provider for purposes of determining whether a transfer of assets is a contribution or an exchange.

In addition to the difficulty in determining if a transaction was an exchange transaction or a contribution, FASB heard there is difficulty in distinguishing between a condition and a restriction, particularly when funds are provided to an NFP with the stipulation of a certain outcome, but no return policy is specified. There is also diversity in practice in determining whether the likelihood of failing to meet a condition is remote, which can change when a contribution is recognized.

The ASU requires NFPs to consider a contribution to be conditional if the agreement includes a barrier that must be overcome and either a right of return of assets transferred or a right of release. The following are indicators of a barrier:

- Measurable performance-related barrier or other measurable barrier
- Limited discretion by the recipient on the conduct of an activity
- Stipulations that are related to the purpose of the agreement

When is this ASU effective?

Effective date — Resource recipient

- Public business entity or an NFP that has issued, or is a conduit bond obligor for, securities that are traded, listed, or quoted on an exchange or an over-the-counter market (OTC): Annual periods beginning after June 15, 2018, including interim periods within those annual periods.
- All other entities: Annual periods beginning after December 15, 2018, and interim periods within annual periods beginning after December 15, 2019.

Effective date — Resource provider

- Public business entity or an NFP that has issued, or is a conduit bond obligor for, securities that are traded, listed, or quoted on an exchange or an OTC market: Annual periods beginning after December 15, 2018, including interim periods within those annual periods.
- All other entities: Annual periods beginning after December 15, 2019, and interim periods within annual periods beginning after December 15, 2020.

Early adoption is permitted. The transition uses a modified prospective basis, but retrospective application is permitted. In the first set of financial statements following the effective date, the amendments should be applied to agreements that are either not completed as of the effective date or entered into after the effective date.

Knowledge check

3. Exchange transactions are when participants receive

    a. Equal value.
    b. Commensurate value.
    c. Equivalent value.
    d. Proportionate value.

4. Which of the following is **not** an indicator of a barrier?

    a. Measurable performance-related barrier or other measurable barrier.
    b. Limited discretion by the recipient on the conduct of an activity.
    c. Stipulations that are related to the purpose of the agreement.
    d. The extent to which a stipulation requires additional action.

ASU No. 2016-02, *Leases (Topic 842)*

ASU No. 2016-02 was issued in February 2016 and creates new FASB Accounting Standards Codification (ASC) 842. Current FASB ASC 840 will be superseded when FASB ASC 842 becomes effective. The process took nearly 10 years to complete and involved a discussion paper and two proposed ASUs.

Why was this ASU issued?

Users of financial statements have criticized the prior lease accounting rules. In particular, users did not feel that operating leases were faithful representations of the transaction. Often cited as "off-balance-sheet" transactions, users felt that companies were manipulating the rules-based accounting by structuring their leases to qualify as operating. This project was intended to provide users the information they felt necessary and while providing preparers with a principles-based approach.

Who is affected by this update?

All entities are within the scope of this ASU. Transactions that are not in the scope include leases of intangible assets; leases to explore for or use minerals, oil, natural gas, and similar nonregenerative resources; leases of biological assets (including timber); leases of inventory, and leases of assets under construction.

What are the main provisions of this ASU?

Definition of a lease

One of the largest changes in this ASU is the definition of a lease. A *lease* is now defined as "a contract, or part of a contract, that conveys the right to control the use of identified property, plant, or equipment (an identified asset) for a period of time in exchange for consideration." You will note from this definition that this ASU heavily borrows from the theories of revenue recognition.

The right to control the use of the asset is critical in the update to the leasing guidance. Control means that the customer has both

- the right to obtain substantially all the economic benefits from the use of the asset, and
- the right to direct the use of the asset.

Economic benefits include using, holding, or subleasing the asset. The economic benefits for use of an asset include its primary output and by-products. A customer has the right to direct the use of an identified asset throughout the period of use if the customer has the right to direct how and for what purpose the asset is used throughout the period of use, or the relevant decisions are predetermined and the customer has the right to operate the asset without the supplier having the right to change those operating instructions, or they designed the asset in a way that predetermines how and for what purpose the asset will be used.

There are essentially three steps to the leasing guidance:

- Step 1 — Determine whether a contract contains a lease.
- Step 2 — Identify the separate lease components within the contract.
- Step 3 — Allocate the consideration in the contract to each separate lease component and nonlease component of the contract.

Step 1 includes looking at substantive substitution rights as well as the decision-making rights of the lessee. Similar to revenue recognition's concept of a performance obligation, step 2 requires the entity to determine if there are separate lease components. A separate component exists if the lessee can benefit from the right of use either on its own or together with other resources that are readily available to the lessee and the right of use is neither highly dependent on nor highly interrelated with the other right(s) to use underlying assets in the contract. Finally, the entity must allocate the consideration on a relative stand-alone price basis to the separate lease components and the nonlease components of the contract. If observable stand-alone prices are not readily available, the NFP should estimate the stand-alone prices. Initial direct costs should be allocated to the separate lease components on the same basis as the lease payments. There is a practical expedient for step 3. NFPs can make an accounting policy election by class of underlying asset, to not separate nonlease components from lease components and instead to account for them as a single lease component. Although this is simpler approach, it is important to note that the size of the liability will be increased under this expedient.

The ASU also addresses the *lease term*. It is defined as the noncancelable period for which a lessee has the right to use an underlying asset, together with all of the following:

- Periods covered by an option to extend the lease if the lessee is reasonably certain to exercise that option
- Periods covered by an option to terminate the lease if the lessee is reasonably certain not to exercise that option
- Periods covered by an option to extend (or not to terminate) the lease in which exercise of the option is controlled by the lessor.

Lessee accounting

Lease classification

Entities must classify each separate lease component at the commencement date as either an operating lease or a finance lease. NFPs would not reassess the lease classification after the commencement date unless the contract is modified, and the modification is not accounted for as a separate contract.

A finance lease is a lease that meets any of the following criteria at lease commencement:

- The lease **transfers ownership** of the underlying asset to the lessee by the end of the lease term.
- The lease grants the lessee an option to purchase the underlying asset that the lessee is **reasonably certain** to exercise.

- The lease term is for the **major part** of the remaining economic life of the underlying asset. However, if the commencement date falls at or near the end of the economic life, this criterion shouldn't be used.
- The present value of the sum of the lease payments and any residual value guaranteed by the lessee equals or exceeds **substantially all** of the fair value of the underlying asset.
- The underlying asset is of such a **specialized nature** that it is expected to have no alternative use to the lessor at the end of the lease term.

It is important to note that, in the implementation guidance, FASB has indicated that if entity's wish to keep the current practice of 75%, 90%, and the like, they can, but are not required to.

An operating lease is any lease other than a finance lease.

The general rule for leases is that an entity would not reassess lease term or lease options unless

- there is a significant event or change that is within the control of the lessee that directly affects whether the lessee is reasonably certain to exercise or not to exercise an option to extend or terminate the lease or to purchase the underlying asset;
- there is an event that is written into the contract that obliges the lessee to exercise (or not to exercise) an option to extend or terminate the lease; or
- the lessee elects to exercise an option even though the entity had previously determined that the lessee was not reasonably certain to and vice versa.

Recognition

All lessees, whether operating or finance leases, should recognize a liability to make lease payments and a right of use asset representing its right to use the underlying asset for the lease term in the statement of financial position.

The lease liability is measured as the present value of lease payments, including fixed payments or in substance fixed payments, less any lease incentives paid or payable to the lessee. The present value calculation should also include the exercise price of an option to purchase the underlying asset if the lessee is reasonably certain to exercise that option. In addition, the liability should include the present value of payments for penalties for terminating the lease as well as amounts probable of being owed by the lessee under residual value guarantees. Variable lease payments that depend on an index or a rate initially measured using the index or rate at the commencement date are also included in the present value calculations. Payments to be made in optional periods should be included only if the lessee is reasonably certain to exercise the option to extend the lease or not to exercise an option to terminate the lease. Finally, optional payments to purchase the underlying asset should be included in the measurement of lease assets and lease liabilities if the lessee is reasonably certain to exercise that purchase option.

Do not include variable lease payments other than those tied to an index or rate (that is, usage-oriented payments or percent rents), any guarantee by the lessee of the lessor's debt, or amounts allocated to nonlease components.

The discount rate for the present value calculation should be the calculated based on the information available at the commencement date. The lessee should use the rate implicit in the lease whenever that rate is readily determinable. If it is not readily determinable, they should use the entities incremental borrowing rate.

The entity should then recognize a corresponding right of use asset. The asset is measured as the sum of the initial measurement of the lease liability plus any lease payments made to the lessor at or before the commencement date, minus any lease incentives received plus any initial direct costs incurred by the lessee.

Lease payments should be remeasured only if any of the following occur:

- The lease is modified, and that modification is not accounted for as a separate contract.
- A contingency is resolved such that some or all of the variable lease payments now meet the definition of lease payments.
- There is a change in any of the following:
  - The lease term
  - The assessment of whether the lessee is reasonably certain to exercise or not to exercise an option to purchase the underlying asset
  - Amounts probable of being owed by the lessee under residual value guarantees

FASB did include a short-term lease exception for leases with a term of 12 months or less (including option periods that are reasonably certain of being exercised). In such a case, a lessee can make an accounting policy election by asset class, to NOT recognize lease assets and lease liabilities and instead recognize lease expense on a straight-line basis over the lease term. Unlike IASB, FASB did not include a small dollar lease exception.

Subsequent measurement — Finance leases

Each period, the lessee should calculate the interest on the lease liability using the appropriate discount rate and balance on the lease liability. The right of use asset is then amortized each period starting at the commencement date and ending at the earlier of the end of the useful life of the right of use asset or the end of the lease term. If the lease transfers ownership to the lessee or the lessee is reasonably certain to exercise an option to purchase the underlying asset, then there is an exception and the lessee should amortize the right-of-use asset to the end of the useful life of the underlying asset. Variable lease payments that were not included in the lease liability will be expensed each period.

The lease liability will be adjusted each period to recognize an increasing in the carrying amount of the lease liability to reflect interest on the lease liability which would be reduced by any payment made during the period. The right of use asset would be presented at cost less any accumulated amortization and any accumulated impairment losses.

Subsequent measurement — Operating leases

Unlike finance leases, operating leases will not recognize interest expense or amortization expense. Instead, they will recognize a single lease cost (lease expense, rent expense, and so on) each period. The single lease cost allocates the total of all remaining lease payments to be made during the lease term over the remaining lease term on a straight-line basis. In addition, variable lease payments that were not included in the lease liability will be expensed each period. Because operating leases will now be recognized on the balance sheet, entities must perform impairment testing and any impairment of the right of use asset should be expensed.

Cash flow

For finance leases, payments of principal will be presented in the financing section of the cash flow statement while interest payments will be presented in the operating section. For operating leases, the entire lease cost will be classified as an operating cash flow.

Presentation and disclosure

Finance lease right of use assets and operating lease right of use assets should be shown separately from each other and from other assets. Finance lease liabilities and operating lease liabilities should also be presented separately from each other and from other liabilities.

ASU No. 2016-02 includes many disclosures. For instance, an organization must include general information about the nature of its leases, including a general description of the lease including terms, conditions, restrictions, and covenants. Lessees should also disclose significant assumptions and judgments including how they determined whether the contract contained a lease as well as the allocation of consideration between lease and nonlease components. Lessees should provide a maturity analysis of its finance lease liabilities and its operating lease liabilities separately, showing the undiscounted cash flows on an annual basis for a minimum of each of the first five years and in total for the remaining years. A reconciliation of the undiscounted cash flows to the finance lease liabilities and operating lease liabilities recognized in the statement of financial position should also be disclosed.

Lessor accounting

Stakeholders were most concerned with lessee accounting and specifically operating leases. As such, FASB decided not to make major changes to lessor accounting. However, some changes were made to conform and align lessor accounting with FASB ASC 606, *Revenue from Contracts with Customers*.

When is this ASU effective?

ASU No. 2019-10, *Financial Instruments — Credit Losses (Topic 326), Derivatives and Hedging (Topic 815), and Leases (Topic 842): Effective Dates*, was issued in November 2019 and deferred the effective date for nonpublic entities. Because *Leases* already is effective for all public entities (that is, including NFP conduit bond obligors), the board retained the effective date for those entities, including SRCs. The board also decided, consistent with having bucket two be at least two years after the initial effective date, to defer the effective date for all other entities by an additional year. Therefore, *Leases* is effective for all other entities for fiscal years beginning after December 15, 2020, and interim periods within fiscal years beginning after December 15, 2021. Early application continues to be allowed.

Key point
A thorough discussion of the full text of ASU No. 2016-02 is beyond the scope of this chapter and this course. Readers are strongly encouraged to read the full update, which is available at www.fasb.org.

Knowledge check

5. Which is an appropriate lease classification under ASU No. 2016-02?

   a. Capital lease.
   b. Finance lease.
   c. Investing lease.
   d. Quasi lease.

6. Operating leases result in the recognition of

   a. Interest expense.
   b. Amortization expense.
   c. A single lease cost.
   d. Depreciation expense.

Other recent FASB standards

ASUs that can affect NFPs

The following ASUs issued by FASB are considered relevant to most NFP entities. Readers should be aware that other ASUs not listed here may apply to them or their clients. Information about ASUs not listed and discussed in this chapter are available at www.fasb.org.

Unless otherwise noted, the standards in the following list may be adopted prior to the effective date and the effective dates listed are those for annual periods of nonpublic business entities. Some of these ASUs have different effective dates for interim reporting than those listed here.

These ASUs are considered relevant to most NFP entities:

- ASU No 2016-13, *Financial Instruments — Credit Losses (Topic 326): Measurement of Credit Losses on Financial Instruments*. This update is effective for fiscal years beginning after December 15, 2020.
- ASU No. 2016-15, *Statement of Cash Flows (Topic 230): Classification of Certain Cash Receipts and Cash Payments (a consensus of the Emerging Issues Task Force)*. This update is effective for fiscal years beginning after December 15, 2018.
- *ASU No. 2016-18, Statement of Cash Flows (Topic 230): Restricted Cash (a consensus of the FASB Emerging Issues Task Force). This update is effective for fiscal years beginning after December 15, 2018.*
- ASU No. 2017-04, *Intangibles — Goodwill and Other (Topic 350): Simplifying the Test for Goodwill Impairment*. This is effective for annual or any interim goodwill impairment tests in fiscal years beginning after December 15, 2021.
- ASU No. 2017-07, *Compensation — Retirement Benefits (Topic 715): Improving the Presentation of Net Periodic Pension Cost and Net Periodic Postretirement Benefit Cost*. This ASU is effective for annual periods beginning after December 15, 2018.
- ASU No. 2017-08, *Receivables — Nonrefundable Fees and Other Costs (Subtopic 310-20): Premium Amortization on Purchased Callable Debt Securities*. This ASU is effective for fiscal years beginning after December 15, 2019.
- ASU No. 2017-10, *Service Concession Arrangements (Topic 853): Determining the Customer of the Operation Services (a consensus of the FASB Emerging Issues Task Force)*. This ASU is effective with the adoption of Topic 606.
- ASU No. 2018-13, *Fair Value Measurement (Topic 820): Disclosure Framework — Changes to the Disclosure Requirements for Fair Value Measurement*. This ASU is effective for fiscal years, and interim periods within those fiscal years, beginning after December 15, 2019.
- ASU No. 2019-03, *Not-for-Profit Entities (Topic 958): Updating the Definition of Collections*. This ASU is effective for fiscal years beginning after December 15, 2019.
- ASU No. 2019-06, *Intangibles — Goodwill and Other (Topic 350), Business Combinations (Topic 805), and Not-for-Profit Entities (Topic 958): Extending the Private Company Accounting Alternatives on Goodwill and Certain Identifiable Intangible Assets to Not-for-Profit Entities*. This ASU was effective upon issuance.
- ASU No. 2019-10, *Financial Instruments — Credit Losses (Topic 326), Derivatives and Hedging (Topic 815), and Leases (Topic 842): Effective Dates.*

ASU No. 2016-13

Why was this ASU issued?

Current GAAP uses an "incurred loss" methodology for recognizing credit losses. This model delays recognition until it is probable a loss has been incurred. The "probable" threshold has caused many issues for preparers because it prevents them from recognizing a loss they expect but has not yet reached the "probable" threshold. This issue was exacerbated by the global financial crisis. In 2008, FASB and IASB established a Financial Crisis Advisory Group (FCAG) to advise the boards on improvements to financial reporting in response to the financial crisis. The FCAG identified delayed loss recognition as a weakness because the delayed recognition of credit losses results in the potential overstatement of assets. The FCAG recommended exploring more forward-looking alternatives to the incurred loss methodology.

Although this ASU will heavily affect the banking industry, NFPs will also be affected because all financial instruments are in the scope of this standard.

Who is affected by this update?

This ASU affects any entities holding financial assets and net investment in leases that are not measured at fair value with changes in fair value running through net income. NFPs that own investments that are classified as held to maturity or any financial asset that are measured at amortized cost (including accounts receivable) will be affected.

What are the main provisions of this ASU?

ASU No. 2016-13 requires a financial asset (or a group of financial assets) measured at amortized cost basis to be presented at the net amount expected to be collected. Entities would then use an allowance for credit losses (valuation account) to present those assets at the amount expected to be collected. The allowance would be updated each balance sheet date and any changes would be run through net income. Credit losses would be measured on newly recognized financial assets, as well as the existing financial assets that experienced changes in credit quality during the period. In addition, instead of using only historical experience, the determination of what is expected would be based on past events, including historical experience, current conditions, and reasonable and supportable forecasts. NFPs will need to use both internal as well as external information to develop their expectations. Entities would need to identify credit quality indicators and monitor the changes in these indicators over the period these assets are held. This will require considerable professional judgment.

When is this ASU effective?

The ASU is effective for all entities (other than SEC filers) for fiscal years beginning after December 15, 2020, and interim periods within fiscal years beginning after December 15, 2021. Early adoption is permitted but not before fiscal years beginning after December 15, 2018, including interim periods within those fiscal years.

Note: ASU No. 2019-10 delayed the effective date for this ASU for all other entities to fiscal years beginning after December 15, 2022, including interim periods within those fiscal years.

Implementation issues

Many NFPs will need to work to develop the data sets to be able to effectively determine the expected credit loss. The delayed effective date was designed to allow entities to accumulate the information needed.

Knowledge check

7. Which investment is **not** affected by ASU No. 2016-13?

    a. Held to maturity debt securities.
    b. Available-for-sale debt securities.
    c. Accounts receivable.
    d. Trading securities.

ASU No. 2016-15

Why was this ASU issued?

ASU No. 2016-15 was issued in response to stakeholder feedback that there was diversity in practice in how certain cash receipts and cash payments were presented and classified in the statement of cash flows. Most ASUs focus on providing recognition and measurement that drive consistent treatment for the balance sheet and income statement. There is typically less guidance on how each transaction should be treated for the statement of cash flows. This has resulted in diversity in practice.

Who is affected by this update?

The ASU applies to all entities, including NFP entities that are required to present a statement of cash flows under FASB ASC 230.

What are the main provisions of this ASU?

The ASU addresses multiple areas including the following:

- Debt prepayment or debt extinguishment costs
- Settlement of zero-coupon debt instruments or other debt instruments with coupon interest rates that are insignificant in relation to the effective interest rate of the borrowing
- Contingent consideration payments made after a business combination
- Proceeds from the settlement of insurance claims
- Proceeds from the settlement of corporate-owned life insurance policies, including bank-owned life insurance policies
- Distributions received from equity method investees
- Beneficial interests in securitization transactions
- Separately identifiable cash flows and application of the predominance principle

We will address the areas that will have the largest impact on NFPs.

Debt prepayment or debt extinguishment costs are paid by a borrower in connection with settling a debt financing arrangement before the maturity date. There are often prepayment penalty provisions. FASB clarified that these payments should be classified as cash outflows for financing activities.

Zero-coupon bonds are typically issued or traded at significant discounts. Unlike typical bonds, interest is not paid throughout the term of the bond. Interest is paid upon maturity. The diversity in practice was created by the determination of whether or not to bifurcate the interest from the principal. FASB clarified that the portion attributable to the accreted interest is cash outflows for operating activities whereas the portion attributable to the principal is deemed as cash outflows for financing activities.

Existing GAAP indicates that proceeds of insurance settlements should be treated as cash inflows from operation with an exception for proceeds directly related to investing or financing activities. FASB received feedback that it was unclear what "directly related to investing or financing activities" means in particular whether it related to the insurance coverage or the planned use. This ASU clarifies that classification of cash proceeds received from the settlement of insurance claims should be based on the related insurance coverage (that is, the nature of the loss). If there is a lump sum settlement, entities would classify based of the nature of each loss included in the settlement.

To prevent having to provide further clarifications for cash flow items, FASB clarified the predominance principle. First entries should apply specific guidance in GAAP. If there is no specific guidance, entities should determine each separately identifiable source or use of cash on the basis of the nature of the underlying cash flows. When the transaction has aspects of more than one class of cash flows and it cannot be separated by source or use, determine the activity that is likely to be the predominant source or use.

When is this ASU effective?

This ASU is effective for all entities other than public business entities, for fiscal years beginning after December 15, 2018, and interim periods within fiscal years beginning after December 15, 2019. Early adoption is permitted, including adoption in an interim period.

Knowledge check

8. Debt extinguishment costs should be presented in which category on the statement of cash flows?

   a. Operating activities.
   b. Investing activities.
   c. Financing activities.
   d. Noncash activity.

ASU No. 2016-18

Why was this ASU issued?

FASB heard from stakeholders that diversity in practice existed in the classification and presentation of changes in restricted cash on the statement of cash flows. Some entities classified transfers between cash and restricted cash accounts as operating, investing, or financing activities, or as a combination of those activities, in the statement of cash flows. In addition, some entities presented cash flows to or from a restricted cash account as cash inflows and cash outflows, whereas others disclosed the transaction as noncash.

Who is affected by this update?

This ASU applies to all entities that have restricted cash or restricted cash equivalents.

What are the main provisions of this ASU?

FASB clarified that the statement of cash flows should present the change during the period in the total of cash, cash equivalents, and amounts generally described as restricted cash or restricted cash equivalents. The statement should reconcile the beginning-of-period and end-of-period total amounts which include restricted cash and restricted cash equivalents. FASB did not define restricted cash. Transfers between cash accounts including restricted cash accounts inflows or outflows as they did not come in or leave the entity and as such are not reported as cash flow activities in the statement of cash flows.

When is this ASU effective?

The ASU is effective for all entities for fiscal years, and interim periods within those fiscal years, beginning after December 15, 2018. Early implementation is permitted.

Implementation issues

Often, restricted cash is not presented with cash and cash equivalents. They can be buried within "other assets" or even shown as a long-term asset. Often, they can be presented in more than one line item. As such, entities will have to identify all restricted cash and cash equivalents and either present on the face of the statement or disclose in the notes, the line items and amounts of where the restricted cash was presented in the balance sheet. Entities will also be required to disclose information about the nature of restrictions on its cash, cash equivalents, and amounts generally described as restricted cash or restricted cash equivalents.

Knowledge check

9. Where should restricted cash transactions be presented?

    a. As either operating, investing or financing cash flows.
    b. Not presented on the cash flow statement.
    c. Disclosed only in the notes.
    d. Presented as a noncash activity.

ASU No. 2017-04

Why was this ASU issued?

In 2014, the Private Company Council and FASB issued a private company alternative to allow private companies an alternative accounting treatment for subsequently measuring goodwill. This alternative was not permitted for NFP entities and public business entities. FASB was then asked to provide the alternative for all entities. FASB decided not to offer the alternative. Instead, it looked for ways to simplify the test for goodwill impairment.

Who is affected by this update?

This ASU is required for public business entities and other entities that have goodwill reported in their financial statements and have not elected the private company alternative for the subsequent measurement of goodwill.

What are the main provisions of this ASU?

Prior to this ASU, the goodwill impairment testing required a two-step process. Step 1 looks to determine if there is goodwill impairment while step 2 determines the amount of impairment. Step 2 requires significant valuation and the calculation of implied goodwill. This ASU removes the requirement to perform step 2, and now impairment would equal the amount by which the carrying amount exceeds the reporting unit's fair value without any calculation of implied goodwill. Entities can still perform a qualitative assessment (sometimes referred to as step 0) if desired.

When is this ASU effective?

NFPs should apply this ASU to their annual or any interim goodwill impairment tests in fiscal years beginning after December 15, 2021. Early adoption is permitted for interim or annual goodwill impairment tests performed on testing dates after January 1, 2017.

Knowledge check

10. ASU No. 2017-04 removed which step in the goodwill impairment testing?

    a. Step 0.
    b. Step 1.
    c. Step 2.
    d. Step 3.

ASU No. 2017-07

Why was this ASU issued?

Pension costs are made up many heterogenous components (service cost, interest cost, and the like). This presentation is not transparent as to the components.

Who is affected by this update?

This ASU applies to all employers that offer defined benefit pension plans, other postretirement benefit plans, or other benefits subject to FASB ASC 715.

What are the main provisions of this ASU?

This ASU requires that service cost be presented with compensation cost and that the remaining components be presented as non-operating. If the other components are presented in a separate line item, they should be appropriately described. However, if a separate line item is not used, the entity must disclose where the components are located. In addition, only the service cost component can be capitalized if it meets the capitalization requirements. The other components are not permitted to be capitalized.

When is this ASU effective?

The ASU is effective for annual periods beginning after December 15, 2018, and interim periods within annual periods beginning after December 15, 2019. Early adoption is permitted.

Knowledge check

11. ASU No. 2017-07 permits the capitalization of which component of pension cost?

    a. Service cost.
    b. Interest cost.
    c. The expected return on plan assets for the period.
    d. The prior service cost or credit component.

ASU No. 2017-08

Why was this ASU issued?

When a debt security is issued at a premium, the premium is amortized over the maturity of the debt. However, when the debt is callable, if the debt is called prior to the maturity date, the unamortized premium is recorded as a loss.

Who is affected by this update?

All entities that hold investments in callable debt securities that were issued at a premium are affected.

What are the main provisions of this ASU?

This ASU requires an entity to amortize the premium to the earliest call date in lieu of the maturity date. Debt instruments issued at a discount are not affected.

When is this ASU effective?

This ASU is effective for fiscal years beginning after December 15, 2019, and interim periods within fiscal years beginning after December 15, 2020. Early adoption is permitted.

Knowledge check

12. A debt security is issued at a premium on January 1, 2017, with a maturity date of December 31, 2026. It is callable on January 1, 2022. The premium should be amortized over how many years?

    a. 1.
    b. 5.
    c. 9.
    d. 10.

ASU No. 2017-10

Why was this ASU issued?

A *service concession arrangement* (SCA) is an arrangement between a grantor (typically a government) and an operating entity (a private entity). An example would be a public toll road owned by the government and a private entity that operates the toll booth.

FASB ASC 853 applies when a public-sector grantor

- controls or has the ability to modify or approve the services that the operating entity must provide with the infrastructure, to whom it must provide them, and at what price; and
- controls — through ownership, beneficial entitlement, or otherwise — any residual interest in the infrastructure at the end of the term of the arrangement.

There was confusion as to whether the customer in an SCA would be the grantor or the third-party users (drivers on the toll road). Determining who the customer is, is very important under FASB ASC 606 because the contract must be with a customer.

Who is affected by this update?

This ASU applies to operating entities in an SCA within the scope of FASB ASC 853.

What are the main provisions of this ASU?

The standard clarifies that the grantor entity, not the third-party users, would be the customer in an SCA. Therefore, the government is the customer of the private operator, not the drivers. Although the drivers are paying the tolls, they are treated as a third-party payer.

When is this ASU effective?

If an NFP has not yet adopted FASB ASC 606, the ASU is effective with the adoption of FASB ASC 606. If the NFP has early adopted FASB ASC 606, the ASU would be effective for fiscal years beginning after December 15, 2018, and interim periods within fiscal years beginning after December 15, 2019.

ASU No. 2018-13

Why was this ASU issued?

The objective and primary focus of the disclosure framework project is to improve the effectiveness of disclosures in notes to financial statements.

What are the main provisions of this ASU?

This ASU modifies disclosure requirements on fair value measurements. Certain current disclosure requirements will be modified or removed from FASB ASC 820, *Fair Value Measurement*. Certain disclosures are being eliminated because they are not consistent with the concepts in the updated Concepts Statement, *Conceptual Framework for Financial Reporting – Chapter 8: Notes to Financial Statements*, or because they are no longer considered useful information.

The following disclosure requirements are removed:

- The amount of and reasons for transfers between level 1 and level 2 of the fair value hierarchy
- The policy for timing of transfers between levels
- The valuation policies and procedures for level 3 fair value measurements
- For nonpublic entities, the change in unrealized gains and losses for the period included in earnings (or changes in net assets) on recurring level 3 fair value measurements held at the end of the reporting period

The following disclosures are modified to align with the Concepts Statement:

- For nonpublic entities, no longer require a reconciliation of the opening balances to the closing balances of recurring level 3 fair value measurements. However, nonpublic entities would be required to disclose transfers into and out of level 3 of the fair value hierarchy and purchases and issues of level 3 assets and liabilities.
- For investments in certain entities that calculate net asset value, require disclosure of the timing of liquidation of an investee's assets and the date when restrictions from redemption will lapse only if the investee has communicated the timing to the entity or announced the timing publicly.
- Clarify the measurement uncertainty disclosure to communicate information about the uncertainty in measurement as of the reporting date rather than information about sensitivity to changes in the future.

ASU No. 2019-03

Why was this ASU issued?

The original definition of a collection in FAS 116 was derived from the American Alliance of Museums' (AAM) Code of Ethics for Museums. When the AAM updated their definition, it created tension for museums where FASB's requirements were more stringent than the AAM.

Who is affected by this update?

Although museums are obviously large users of the concept of collections, any entity who uses collection accounting can apply the updated definition including botanical gardens, libraries, aquariums, arboretums, historic sites, planetariums, zoos, art galleries, nature, science, and technology centers.

What are the main provisions of this ASU?

When an item meets the definition of a collection item, GAAP permits the entity to not capitalize it. This assists with donations of works of art and the like that would be near impossible and expensive to value. There were three requirements to qualify to be a collection item. ASU No. 2019-03 updates the third to permit the use of proceeds from sale of a collection item to be used for the "direct care" of existing collection items in addition to the current requirement that it be used for acquisition of more collection items. FASB did not define direct care.

If the NFP does use the proceeds for direct care, the entity would be required to provide their definition for direct care in the notes to the financial statements. Entities must describe their policy for deaccessioning as not all entities would be willing to use the funds for direct care.

When is this ASU effective?

This ASU is effective for annual financial statements issued for fiscal years beginning after December 15, 2019, and for interim periods within fiscal years beginning after December 15, 2020. Early adoption is permitted.

> The AICPA issued a Technical Q&A document in Section 6140 to provide guidance on the term direct care. See paragraph 27 of the Technical Q&A for more information.

ASU No. 2019-06

Why was this ASU issued?

In 2014, the PCC and FASB issued ASU No. 2014-02 that permitted private companies to amortize their goodwill for a period of up to 10 years. In ASU No. 2014-18, certain identifiable intangible assets were permitted to be lumped into goodwill and amortized in lieu of being recognized separately. These exceptions for private companies were provided due to the cost and complexity of the goodwill impairment testing. However, nonprofits are not in the scope of the PCC and were excluded from these standards. Nonprofits have felt that an impairment testing-only option costs do not outweigh the benefits and they sought similar reprieve.

Who is affected by this update?

All entities who meet the definition of an NFP entity per the ASC's Master Glossary.

What are the main provisions of this ASU?

Although FASB continues to debate the proper treatment of goodwill for all entities, as a stopgap, they have decided to extend the private company exceptions to NFP entities. As such, nonprofits can now amortize their goodwill for a period of up to 10 years and lump customer related intangibles that are not capable of being sold separately and noncompete agreements into goodwill (so long as they choose to amortize goodwill). They would be required to test for impairment only when a triggering event occurs and then have the option to perform the testing at either the reporting unit or organization level.

> FASB continues to evaluate goodwill impairment testing and in 2019 issued an Invitation to Comment (ITC). Nonprofits are expected to be in the scope of any standard setting that comes from the ITC so nonprofits should continue to monitor the projects status.

When is this ASU effective?

The standard is effective upon issuance. However, similar to private companies in ASU No. 2016-03, the standard permits a one-time opt in at any time without requiring a preferability analysis. Once an entity opts in, any future changes would require analysis.

ASU No. 2019-10

Why was this ASU issued?

FASB received considerable feedback from private companies and nonprofits that they did not have sufficient time to adopt the very large projects that were coming successively each year. During outreach, the FASB learned of the many difficulties that private companies and nonprofits face from resource restrictions, technology issues and internal controls structures.

Who is affected by this update?

All nonprofits are eligible for the delay for hedging and current expected credit loss (CECL). However, only nonprofits without conduit debt will receive a delay for leases.

What are the main provisions of this ASU?

FASB recognizes that some projects are larger than others and require significant effort to adopt. The Private Company Decision-Making Framework indicated a one-year delay between public and private. ASU No. 2019-10 updates this concept such than when a project is deemed to be "major" that a two-year delay would be deemed to be appropriate. In addition, an extra year was granted in effective date for ASU No. 2016-13 (the CECL model), and ASU No. 2017-12 (hedging) as well as their related amendments. For ASU No. 2016-02, only nonprofits without conduit debt would receive the extra year pushing back the effective date to calendar years 2021 and fiscal years ending in 2022.

Staff Q&A on whether private companies and NFP entities can apply Staff Accounting Bulletin (SAB) No. 118

In December 2017, the 2017 Tax Cuts and Jobs Act (act) was signed into law. The impact of this law is far reaching for NFP entities. Upon issuance, the SEC issued SAB No. 118, which provided guidance on the application of FASB ASC 740 on income taxes in the reporting period that includes the date on which the act was signed into law. The SEC does not write guidance for nonpublic entities, including NFP entities. However, in January 2018, FASB staff issued a Staff Q&A, which indicated that if an NFP entity applies SAB No. 118, it should apply all relevant aspects of the SAB in its entirety and apply appropriate disclosures.

Relevant outstanding exposure drafts

As of January 2019, there were a number of outstanding exposure documents open for comment as well as exposure documents for which the comment period had closed. Those exposure drafts that are considered relevant to most NFP entities, and their current status, are discussed in the following paragraphs.

> Readers are encouraged to follow the status of these exposure drafts and other outstanding projects at www.fasb.org.

Simplifying the balance sheet classification of debt

The proposed ASU proposes a principle-based approach for determining whether a debt arrangement should be classified as current or noncurrent.

An entity would classify the debt as noncurrent if the liability is contractually due to be settled more than one year after the balance sheet date or the entity has a contractual right to defer settlement of the liability for at least one year (or operating cycle, if longer) after the balance sheet date. The criteria would have to be **as of** the balance sheet date. There is an exception for debt covenant violations with waivers. However, an entity would be required to separately present the liabilities that are classified as noncurrent due to a waiver. One of the most significant changes would be short-term debt that is refinanced on a long-term basis after the balance sheet date because the refinancing did not exist at the date of the balance sheet but arose after that date (a nonrecognized subsequent event).

In 2019, the project was re-exposed, and a final ASU is expected in 2020.

ASU No. 2016-14

ASU No. 2016-14, *Not-for-Profit Entities (Topic 958): Presentation of Not-for-Profit Financial Statements*, was effective for annual financial statements issued for fiscal years beginning after December 15, 2017. Although the standard primarily addresses presentation and disclosures and adoption was pretty smooth, there continues to be much confusion regarding two key areas: equity transfers and functional expenses.

Equity transfers

A recipient entity reports an equity transaction as a separate line item in its statement of activities. A resource provider reports an equity transaction as a separate line in its statement of activities if it specifies an affiliate as beneficiary.

A transfer of assets to a recipient entity is an equity transaction if all of the following conditions are met:

- The resource provider specifies itself or its affiliate as the beneficiary,
- The resource provider and the recipient entity are financially interrelated entities, and
- Neither the resource provider nor its affiliate expects payment of the transferred assets, although payment of investment return on the transferred assets may be expected.

If a resource provider specifies itself as beneficiary, it shall report an equity transaction as an interest in the net assets of the recipient entity (or as an increase in a previously recognized interest).

Equity transfers are reported separately as changes in net assets and do not result in any step-up in basis of the underlying assets transferred. However, a service received from personnel of an affiliate that directly benefits the recipient NFP and for which the affiliate does not charge the recipient NFP may be recorded at the fair value of that service recording a service received from personnel of an affiliate at the cost recognized by the affiliate for the personnel providing that service will significantly overstate or understate the value of the service received.

An equity transaction involves a financially interrelated party either as a third party in a transfer from an entity to one of its affiliates or as a counterparty in a transfer from an entity to itself. In addition, an equity transaction — unlike an equity transfer — is reciprocal; the NFP or its affiliate named as the beneficiary receives an ongoing economic interest in the assets held by the recipient entity.

The increase in net assets associated with services received from personnel of an affiliate that directly benefit the recipient NFP and for which the affiliate does not charge the recipient NFP are reported as an equity transfer regardless of whether those services are received from personnel of a not-for-profit affiliate or any other affiliate. The corresponding decrease in net assets or the creation or enhancement of an asset resulting from the use of services received from personnel of an affiliate is reported similar to how other such expenses or assets are reported.

Functional expenses

Under ASU No. 2016-14, all NFPs must report information about all expenses in one location — on the face of the statement of activities, as a schedule in the notes to financial statements, or in a separate financial statement.

The relationship between functional classification and natural classification for all expenses must be presented in an analysis that disaggregates functional expense classifications, such as major classes of program services and supporting activities by their natural expense classifications, such as salaries, rent, electricity, supplies, interest expense, depreciation, awards and grants to others, and professional fees. To the extent that expenses are reported by other than their natural classification (such as salaries included in cost of goods sold or facility rental costs of special events reported as direct benefits to donors), they are reported by their natural classification in the functional expense analysis. For example, salaries, wages, and fringe benefits that are included as part of the cost of goods sold on the statement of activities shall be included with other salaries, wages, and fringe benefits in the functional expense analysis. The level of disaggregation has created some confusion in implementation.

External and direct internal investment expenses that have been netted against investment return shall not be included in the functional expense analysis. Certain items like unrealized gains and losses from available-for-sale debt securities that are typically reported in other comprehensive income of for-profit entities are considered gains or losses and, like other gains and losses, are not included in the functional expense analysis.

Appendix 2A

REVENUE RECOGNITION CASE STUDY

Part 1 — For each of the following scenarios, indicate whether the contract is a contribution or an exchange transaction.

Scenario 1

NFP University is a large research university with a cancer research center. It regularly conducts research to discover more effective methods of treating breast cancer and often receives contributions to support its efforts. The university receives resources from Pharma Inc., a publicly traded entity, to finance the costs of a clinical trial of an experimental cancer drug the pharmaceutical entity developed. Pharma Inc. specifies the protocol of the testing, including the number of participants to be tested, the dosages to be administered, and the frequency and nature of follow-up examinations. The pharmaceutical entity requires a detailed report of the test outcome within two months of the test's conclusion. Additionally, the rights to the results of the study belong to Pharma Inc.

Scenario 2

Jane Hoya is enrolled at CPA University. Jane's total tuition charged for the semester is $45,000. She receives a grant in the amount of $20,000 to use toward tuition, which is paid directly by the federal government to CPA University.

Scenario 3

Happy County provided funding to Motion NFP to perform a research study on the risks and benefits of electric scooters. The agreement requires Motion NFP to plan the study, perform the research, and summarize and submit the research to the local government. The county retains all rights to the study.

Scenario 4

ReSurch University applied for and was awarded a grant from the federal government. The university must follow the Uniform Guidance. ReSurch University is required to incur qualifying expenses to be entitled to the assets and any unspent money during the grant period is forfeited. Additionally, the university is required to return any advanced funding that does not have related qualifying expenses. ReSurch University is required to submit a summary of research findings to the federal government, but the university retains the rights to the findings and has permission to publish the findings if it desires.

Part 2 — For each scenario, determine whether the stipulation is a restriction or a condition.

Scenario 1

Good Causes Foundation gives Workvets (an NFP) a grant in the amount of $200,000 to provide specific career training to disabled veterans. The grant requires Workvets to provide training to at least 4,000 disabled veterans during the next calendar year (1,000 during each quarter), with specific minimum targets that must be met each quarter. Good Causes Foundation specifies a right of release from the obligation in the agreement that it will provide $50,000 each quarter only if Workvets demonstrates that minimum targets are met during the quarter. Workvets routinely provides services to 2,000 disabled veterans a month.

Scenario 2

Sealand Grace is a hospital that has a research program. Sealand Grace receives a $300,000 grant from a federal awarding agency to fund diabetes research. The terms of the grant specify that the hospital must incur certain qualifying expenses in compliance with Uniform Guidance. The grant is paid on a cost-reimbursement basis with Sealand Grace initiating drawdowns of the grant assets. Any unused assets are forfeited and any unallowed costs that have been drawn down by the hospital must be refunded.

Scenario 3

ECO Watch is a public charity that performs research on the impact of invasive species on sensitive local ecosystems, as part of its overall mission to promote a healthy environment. It receives a $200,000 grant from a foundation to perform research on the impact of Asian Carp in the Great Lakes. The grant agreement includes a right of return as part of the foundation's standard wording and a requirement that at the end of the grant period a report must be filed with the foundation that explains how the assets were spent.

Scenario 4

The PAWS Foundation receives a grant proposal from a feline adoption center, which requests a two-year grant in the amount of $200,000 upfront to be used to expand its operations. The agreement indicates that the adoption center must expand its facility by at least 2,000 square feet to accommodate additional cats by the end of the grant period. The grant contains a right of return if the minimum expansion target is not achieved.

Scenario 5

Accountown University is conducting a capital campaign to build a new building to house its school of business and make capital improvements to other existing buildings on campus, including major roof repairs and upgrades to the communications network. Accountown University receives an upfront grant in the amount of $50,000 from a foundation as part of its capital campaign. The agreement contains a right of return requiring that the assets be reimbursed to the resource provider if they are not used for the purposes outlined in the capital campaign solicitation materials.

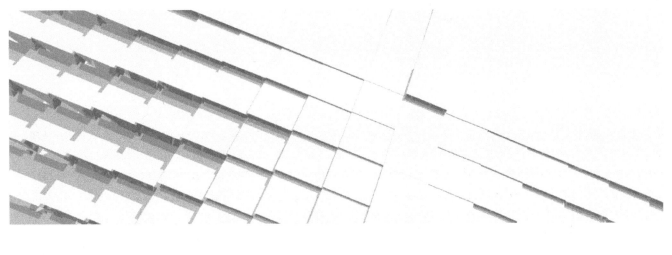

Chapter 3

Federal Government Activities

Learning objectives

- Recognize key changes found in *Government Audtiting Standards, 2018 Revision*.

- Identify the role of the *Compliance Supplement* in a Uniform Guidance compliance audit.

- Identify and apply guidance found in the Uniform Guidance.

- Recognize proposed changes to the Uniform Guidance.

Government Auditing Standards, 2018 Revision

In July 2018, the U.S. Government Accountability Office (GAO) issued *Government Auditing Standards, 2018 Revision* (2018 revision). Upon its effective date, the 2018 revision will supersede the *Government Auditing Standards, 2011 Revision*. The effective date of the 2018 revision is for financial audits, attestation engagements, and reviews of financial statements for periods ending on or after June 30, 2020, and for performance audits beginning on or after July 1, 2019. Therefore, the first full fiscal year audits performed under the 2018 revision will be for June 30, 2020, year-ends. Access to the 2018 revision is available on the GAO website at www.gao.gov/yellowbook/overview. Key changes found in the 2018 revision follow.

Format and organization. One important change relates to the format and organization of the content. The 2018 revision presents all requirements within a box, with the application guidance following. This allows for clear identification of the requirements versus application guidance. Furthermore, two chapters were added and content within chapters has been reorganized. Application guidance has been added to a number of topics. In addition, content that previously was in the appendixes to the 2011 revision, or the current GAO CPE guidance document addressing common CPE questions, has either been incorporated into the 2018 revision or removed.

Independence. This area is one that has some of the more significant changes, particularly as it relates to nonaudit services. For example, the 2018 revision states that auditors should conclude that preparing financial statements in their entirety from a client provided trial balance or underlying accounting records creates significant threats to an auditor's independence. For this type of nonaudit service, auditors should document the threats and safeguards applied to eliminate and reduce threats to an acceptable level or decline to perform the service.

The 2018 revision also states that auditors should identify as threats to independence certain other services related to preparing accounting records and financial statements. Included in this list are

- recording transactions for which management has determined or approved the appropriate account classification, or posting coded transaction to an audited entity's general ledger;
- preparing certain line items or sections of the financial statements based on information in the trial balance;
- posting entries that an audited entity's management has approved to the entity's trial balance; and
- preparing account reconciliations that identify reconciling items for the audited entity management's evaluation.

Auditors should evaluate the significance of threats to independence created by providing the services listed previously and should document the evaluation of the significance of such threats.

The 2018 Yellow Book includes two flowcharts at the end of chapter 3 that further illustrate the independence requirements. Figure 1, "Generally Accepted Government Auditing Standards Conceptual Framework for Independence," is a flowchart that auditors use when applying the conceptual framework in accordance with *Government Auditing Standards* to address threats to independence. Figure 1 refers the user to figure 2, "Independence Considerations for Preparing Accounting Records and Financial Statements," for independence considerations regarding those specific nonaudit services. The flowcharts are a good tool to assist auditors in understanding the requirements around independence.

Overall, there is increased emphasis in the 2018 revision regarding the consideration of nonaudit services by the auditor. This is an area that needs to be considered early on because an auditor is required to be independent from an audited entity during any period of time that falls within the period covered by the financial statements or subject matter of the engagement and the period of the professional engagement. For example, an auditor performing nonaudit services related to a June 30, 2020, financial statement audit (the first full fiscal year required to be audited under the 2018 Yellow Book), the auditor is required to be independent beginning July 1, 2019.

> ### *Government Auditing Standards, 2018 Revision* — Independence alert
>
> An auditor must be independent from the audited entity for the entire period under audit. Therefore, for a June 30, 2020, fiscal year-end, an auditor is required to comply with the 2018 Yellow Book independence requirements beginning July 1, 2019.

CPE. The application guidance for CPE emphasizes the need to obtain CPE related to *Government Auditing Standards*, particularly in a year where the standards have been revised. In addition, as noted previously, certain guidance found in GAO's 2005 document "Guidance on GAGAS Requirements for Continuing Professional Education," has been included as application guidance in the 2018 revision. Upon the effective date of the 2018 revision that document will be retired.

Peer review. The content related to peer review has been expanded, and includes a listing of recognized peer review organizations. The 2018 revision notes that audit organizations affiliated with a recognized peer review organization should comply with their requirements and certain other requirements found in the 2018 revision.

Waste and abuse. The 2011 revision of *Government Auditing Standards* included auditor requirements related to abuse. The 2018 revision moves the concept of abuse to application guidance, and adds the concept of waste.

Reviews of financial statements. The 2018 revision added guidance related to reviews of financial statements.

Performance audits. The content related to performance audits now includes considerations for when internal control is significant to the audit objectives.

OMB *Compliance Supplement*

The *Compliance Supplement*, updated yearly, is one of the most important sources of guidance for the auditor performing single audits. The supplement identifies the types of compliance requirements that the Office of Management and Budget (OMB) and the federal agencies expect to be considered as part of a single audit. It provides information for the purpose of understanding federal program objectives, procedures, and compliance requirements as well as the audit objectives and suggested audit procedures for the programs included in the supplement.

Occasionally, the *Compliance Supplement* undergoes an update that is more extensive than the usual yearly update. The 2019 *Compliance Supplement*, which was effective for June 30, 2019, and forward fiscal years, was such an update. The 2019 Supplement was first issued in July 2019. However, due to the number and extent of changes, there were many errors and inconsistencies found in the supplement. Therefore, in September 2019, OMB issued an updated version addressing many of the larger errors.

The 2020 *Compliance Supplement* was not available when this course was being updated. The content here is based on prior years' supplements. Auditors are cautioned to carefully evaluate the revisions made to the 2020 *Compliance Supplement*, which are applicable to June 30, 2020, and forward year-end audits.

The *Compliance Supplement* includes the following:

- Part 1 — Background, Purpose, and Applicability
- Part 2 — Matrix of Compliance Requirements
- Part 3 — Compliance Requirements
- Part 4 — Agency Program Requirements
- Part 5 — Clusters of Programs
- Part 6 — Internal Control
- Part 7 — Guidance for Auditing Programs Not Included in this *Compliance Supplement*
- Appendixes

The general information provided subsequently is based on the 2019 *Compliance Supplement*. The following sections of the *Compliance Supplement* are updated each year for new or revised information:

- Part 2, identifies the types of compliance requirements that have been identified as subject to audit for the programs included in the Supplement..
- Part 3 lists and describes the compliance requirements, the audit objectives, and the suggested audit procedures. (See the note below regarding part 3.1 and 3.2.)
- Part 4 discusses program objectives, program procedures, and compliance requirements that are specific for each federal program included in the *Compliance Supplement*. For example, for a particular program it will specifically identify what eligilbility means for that program. Each year, the update to this part adds and deletes programs and makes changes to a number of existing programs due to regulatory or other changes. Not all programs are included in part 4. For those included, part 3 is required to be used along with part 4. If a program is not included in part 4, the auditor should use part 7.

- Part 5 provides compliance requirements, audit objectives, and suggested audit procedures for the Student Financial Assistance and Research and Development clusters. Clusters are updated and new clusters are identified in this section.
- Part 6 received significant updates in 2019. These changes were done in conjunction with the AICPA's Government Audit Quality Center (GAQC). The 2019 *Compliance Supplement* added two appendixes to part 6.
  - Appendix 1, Illustrative Entity-Wide Controls, provides illustrations of entity-wide controls over compliance for four of the five components of internal control and their related principles as described in the Green Book.
  - Appendix 2, Illustrative Specific Controls for Control Activities, provides specific controls over compliance for control activities that apply to individual types of compliance requirements.
  - The appendix also addresses common confusions around the difference between a process and a control.
  - For each compliance requirement, the appendix provides examples (in a tabular format) of ways entities could design a control that meets the control objective for the requirement.
  - It also addresses IT controls and demonstrates how entities can implement controls through policies.
  - Due to the high deficiency rate in this area, firms should spend time reviewing these examples when considering the design and testing of internal controls.
- Part 7 provides guidance to auditors in both identifying the compliance requirements and designing tests of compliance with such requirements for programs not included in the Supplement.
- Part 8 covers the appendixes. Important appendixes to review include
  - Appendix III, *Federal Agency Single Audit, Key Management Liason, and Program Contacts*, provides information on responsible single audit contacts, key management liasons, and program contacts for each program/cluster included in the Supplement and
  - Appendix V, *List of Changes for the 2019 Compliance Supplement*, provides a list of the changes from the 2017 and 2018 Supplements.
- Appendix VII, *Other Audit Advisories*, includes the administrative relief for grantees impacted in 2017 by Hurricanes Harvey, Irma, or Maria; the effect of the National Defense Authorization Acts (NDAA) of 2017 and 2018; and guidance on audit sampling.
- Appndix VIII, *Examinations of EBT Service Organizations*, provides guidance on audits of state electronic benefits transfer (EBT) service providers (service organizations) regarding the issuance, redemption, and settlement of benefits under the Supplemental Nutrition Assistance Program (CFDA 10.551) in accordance with the American Institute of Certified Public Accountants (AICPA) Statement on Standards for Attestation Engagements (AT) Section 801, *Reporting on Controls at a Service Organization*.
- Appendix IX, *Compliance Supplement Core Team*, lists the team members responsible for the production of the Supplement.

Note: Recent compliance supplements have included two sections of part 3, *Compliance Requirements*. Part 3.1 is used for awards subject to the circulars (pre-Uniform Guidance administrative requirements and cost principles). Part 3.2 is used for auditing federal awards subject to the Uniform Guidance administrative requirements and cost principles. It is important to use the correct part 3 (3.1 or 3.2) for a particular award.

Key point
Be sure to use the version of the supplement that corresponds with the entity's year-end. For example, the 2020 *Compliance Supplement* must be used for June 30, 2020, year-ends and forward. Year-ends prior to that date (for example, a May 31, 2020, year-end) are required to use the 2019 *Compliance Supplement*.

Types of compliance requirements

The 12 types of compliance requirements found in the *Compliance Supplement* are as follows:

A — Activities Allowed or Unallowed

B — Allowable Costs/Cost Principles

C — Cash Management

D — Reserved

E — Eligibility

F — Equipment and Real Property Management

G — Matching, Level of Effort, Earmarking

H — Period of Performance

I — Procurement and Suspension and Debarment

J — Program Income

K — Reserved

L — Reporting

M — Subrecipient Monitoring

N — Special Tests and Provisions

2019 *Compliance Supplement*

In 2019, the *Compliance Supplement* was updated to reflect that federal agencies were required to limit the number of compliance requirements subject to audit to six with the exception of the Research and Development cluster which was permitted to identify seven. For this purpose, the requirements relating to A. Activities Allowed and Unallowed and B. Allowable Costs and Cost Principles are treated as one requirement. When reviewing the matrix for compliance requirements, the Y no longer means "applicable." Instead, Y stands for subject to audit. That means that there may be compliance requirements that are applicable to the program but are not subject to testing in that year. The items that were changed from the prior year were denoted in yellow. Also, note that the columns for requirements D and K were removed in 2019.

When a compliance requirement has been identified as not being subject to audit, the auditor is not prohibited from expanding audit procedures if the terms of a grant award document specify that the additional compliance requirements are material to the administration of the program or if the auditor is aware of additional information that would lead the auditor to believe there are increased risks of fraud, waste, or abuse of federal program funds.

Impact of the 6 — Requirement Mandate

The AICPA received several questions about how the change to a six-requirement maximum would impact reporting on compliance. In September 2019, they addressed these questions in Q&A Section 9110, Special Reports.

Opining on Compliance When the OMB Compliance Supplement Excludes Direct and Material Compliance Requirements From the Scope of a Single Audit

Inquiry — For a single audit performed using a supplement, such as the 2019 Supplement, that limits the number of compliance requirements federal agencies can select as subject to the compliance audit, can an auditor provide an opinion on compliance if the supplement excludes certain types of compliance requirements from the scope of the audit and the auditor is aware that one or more of those excluded requirements could have a direct and material effect on a major federal program? For example, if the supplement does not identify eligibility (one of the 12 potential types of compliance requirements identified in the supplement) as one of the types of compliance requirements subject to the compliance audit for a major federal program, can the auditor provide an opinion on compliance if the auditor is aware that a key part of the program is based on providing benefits to individuals that meet certain income eligibility criteria?

Reply — Yes. Paragraph .29 of AU-C section 935 indicates the auditor should form an opinion at the level specified by the governmental audit requirement. The governmental audit requirement in this case is the supplement, which specifies the compliance requirements to be considered by the auditor. Therefore, the auditor is able to provide an opinion on compliance.

Effect on Auditor Reporting Due to the OMB Compliance Supplement *Change in Approach for Identifying the Requirements Subject to the Single Audit*

Inquiry — Does the change of approach in the supplement for identifying the types of compliance requirements subject to the compliance audit require the auditor to revise the report wording for the report on compliance for each major federal program illustrated in AICPA Audit Guide Government Auditing Standards and Single Audits?

Reply — No. Paragraph .30cii of AU-C section 935 indicates the auditor should include in an introductory paragraph of the auditor's report the "identification of the applicable compliance requirements or a reference to where they can be found." AU-C section 935 defines applicable compliance requirements as "compliance requirements that are subject to the compliance audit." AICPA Audit Guide *Government Auditing Standards* and Single Audits contains illustrative auditor's reports, the introductory paragraphs of which refer to an audit of compliance "with the types of compliance requirements described in the OMB *Compliance Supplement* that could have a direct and material effect" on each of the major federal programs. This wording meets the requirements of AU-C section 935 as it provides a reference to where a report user can find the requirements identified as subject to the compliance audit.

Including an Other-Matter Paragraph to Describe the OMB Compliance Supplement Change in Approach for Identifying the Requirements Subject to the Single Audit

Inquiry — May an auditor include an other-matter paragraph in the report on compliance for each major federal program describing the change to the supplement for identifying the types of compliance requirements subject to the compliance audit?

Reply — Yes. There is nothing to preclude an auditor from including an other-matter paragraph in the report to communicate information about the change to the supplement. If the auditor considers it necessary to communicate this information, the auditor should do so in a paragraph in the auditor's report with the heading "Other Matter" or other appropriate heading as described in AU-C section 706, *Emphasis-of-Matter Paragraphs and Other-Matter Paragraphs in the Independent Auditor's Report.*

See the Technical Questions and Answers at https://www.aicpa.org/content/dam/aicpa/interestareas/frc/downloadabledocuments/tqa-sections/tqa-section-9110-24-27.pdf

The 2019 *Compliance Supplement* can be found at https://www.whitehouse.gov/wp-content/uploads/2019/09/2-CFR_Part-200_Appendix-XI_Compliance-Supplement_August-2019_FINAL_v2_09.19.19.pdf.As a public service, the GAQC has broken the 2019 Supplement down by individual sections. These sections were excerpted from the full PDF file posted on the OMB website. You can access it on the GAQC OMB 2019 *Compliance Supplement* web page at https://www.aicpa.org/interestareas/governmentalauditquality/resources/singleaudit/2019-omb-compliance-supplement.html.

Important!
Auditors are cautioned to carefully evaluate the revisions made to the 2020 *Compliance Supplement*, which are applicable to June 30, 2020, and forward year-end audits.

NDAA

Appendix 7 addresses implementation issues with the timing of the NDAA of 2017 and 2018. Although the NDAA of 2017 was enacted on December 23, 2016, it has not been codified in the Federal Acquisition Regulations. An official OMB memorandum M-18-18 for the micro-purchase threshold provisions was issued by OMB on June 20, 2018, that clarified the effective date for the higher threshold and the approval process for the applicable recipients requesting a micro-purchase threshold higher than $10,000. In spite of the memo, there was some confusion about whether the act was effective on December 23, 2016, or whether only effective once codified in the Federal Acquisition Regulations. Therefore, auditors are not expected to develop audit findings for covered entities that implemented increased purchase thresholds after December 23, 2016, as long as the entity documented the decision in its internal procurement policies. The provisions of NDAA of 2018 will not be effective until they are codified in the Federal Acquisition Regulations. However, in accordance with OMB M-18-18, early implementation is allowed if the grant recipient requests and receives approval from the federal agencies. However, there is some confusion from the grant community about whether the language in the memo allows grant recipients to use the higher thresholds without an official approval from the federal cognizant agency for indirect cost rates. Therefore, auditors are not expected to develop audit findings for grant recipients that implemented increased purchase thresholds after June 20, 2018, as long as the entity documented the decision in its internal procurement policies.

AICPA GAQC *Compliance Supplement* practice tips

The AICPA GAQC (www.aicpa.org/gaqc) has assembled a list of tips for using the *Compliance Supplement*. The following information is derived from that list.

	Practice tips for using the *Compliance Supplement*
1	Be sure you are using the version of the supplement that is effective for the year under audit.
2	As part of your single audit engagement team preparation, hold a planning meeting to review the applicable *Compliance Supplement* with your audit team. Focus the review on the programs to be audited and any significant changes made to the supplement from the prior year. Appendix V of the supplement is particularly useful in identifying the changes made each year. Appendix VII should be a key part of the discussion this year as well.
3	The matrix of compliance requirements in part 2 identifies the compliance requirements that are applicable to the programs included in the supplement. Many issues with using this part of the supplement have been noted in single audit quality reviews. It is important that you use it correctly. Remember that even though a "Y" within the matrix indicates that a compliance requirement is subject to audit, it may not apply at a particular entity because either that entity does not have activity subject to that type of compliance requirement or the activity does not have a material effect on a major program. Therefore, you need to exercise professional judgment when determining which compliance requirements marked "Y" need to be tested at a particular nonfederal entity. Use part 2 appropriately by ■ using professional judgment; ■ assessing each compliance requirement individually; ■ considering both quantitative and qualitative materiality when deciding whether an "applicable" compliance requirement is material to a major program; and ■ documenting the determination of why an applicable requirement is not deemed direct and material. Just using an "n/a" or "not direct and material" tick mark is not enough. You need to document your logic for making the decision.
4	Because parts 4 and 5 of the supplement do not include guidance for all types of compliance requirements that pertain to a program (see introduction to part 4 for additional information), you should use those parts in conjunction with parts 2 and 3.
5	Refrain from using the supplement as a de facto audit program. Remember that the supplement includes "suggested" audit procedures. Auditor judgment is necessary to determine whether the suggested audit procedures are sufficient to achieve the stated audit objectives or whether additional or alternative audit procedures are needed. Therefore, you should *not* consider the supplement to be a "safe harbor" for identifying the audit procedures to apply in a particular engagement. A good understanding of your client is necessary to be sure you are performing the correct procedures for your client's facts and circumstances. Also, you should understand the various federal programs that your client receives to determine whether modifications to the audit approach are necessary.

Uniform Guidance refresher

Title 2 U.S. *Code of Federal Regulations* (CFR) Part 200, *Uniform Administrative Requirements, Cost Principles, and Audit Requirements for Federal Awards* (Uniform Guidance) establishes uniform cost principles and audit requirements for federal awards to nonfederal entities and administrative requirements for all federal grants and cooperative agreements. All guidance for federal agencies and nonfederal entities and their auditors is in the Uniform Guidance in the following sections of Part 200.

A nonfederal entity is required to have a single audit (or program-specific) if it expends $750,000 or more of federal awards in a fiscal year.

Summary of Uniform Guidance subparts

Subpart A, Acronyms and definitions (200.0–200.99)

Subpart A contains the various acronyms and definitions used in the document.

Subpart B, General provisions (200.100–200.113)

Subpart B explains the purpose, applicability, and effective date of the Uniform Guidance. A table in this subpart indicates which subparts are applicable to different types of awards. This table specifies the subparts that are applicable (or not applicable) to a particular type of federal award. Among the types of federal awards noted in the table are grant agreements, cooperative agreements, cost-reimbursement contracts, fixed amount awards, agreements for loans and loan guarantees, interest subsidies, and insurance. It is noted that the requirements established apply to all federal agencies that make federal awards to nonfederal entities, and that the requirements are applicable to all costs related to federal awards.

Subpart C, Pre-federal award requirements and contents of federal awards (200.200–200.213)

Subpart C provides information to federal agencies on information that is required to be provided to nonfederal entities related to applying for and receiving federal awards. This includes determining the type of instrument to be used (for example, grant agreement, cooperative agreement, or contract), and a listing of information that must be included in a federal award document. In addition, this subpart provides guidance to federal agencies regarding reviewing proposals, including evaluating risks posed by applicants.

Subpart D, Post federal award requirements standards for financial and program management (200.300–200.345)

Subpart D contains information for both federal agencies and nonfederal entities regarding their responsibilities after a federal award is granted. It covers a wide range of topics. Auditors should identify and understand the content that relates to nonfederal entities because it will be one basis for compliance testing of awards, or increments of awards, subject to the Uniform Guidance.

Topic areas covered in Subpart D are as follows:

- Standards for financial and program management
- Property standards
- Procurement standards
- Performance and financial monitoring and reporting
- Subrecipient monitoring and management
- Record retention and access
- Remedies for noncompliance
- Closeout
- Post-closeout adjustments and continuing responsibilities
- Collection of amounts due

Subpart E, Cost principles (200.400–200.475)

Subpart E contains information regarding cost principles for federal awards previously found in the cost circulars. These principles must be used in determining the allowable costs of work performed by the nonfederal entity under federal awards. These principles also must be used by the nonfederal entity as a guide in the pricing of fixed-price contracts and subcontracts where costs are used in determining the appropriate price.

Subpart F, Audit requirements (200.500–200.521)

Subpart F sets forth the requirements for auditors performing Uniform Guidance compliance audits of nonfederal entities expending federal awards.

Uniform Guidance appendixes

There are a number of appendixes to the Uniform Guidance on a wide variety of subjects. Some of the appendixes contain detailed information on the subject, and others are references to material located elsewhere. Of special note are the following appendixes, some of which reference other guidance and requirements related to a single audit:

- Appendix I, *Full Text of Notice of Funding Opportunity*
- Appendix IX, *Hospital Cost Principles* – The Hospital Cost Principles appendix has not been updated. The existing principles located at 45 CFR Part 74 Appendix E, entitled "Principles for Determining Cost Applicable to Research and Development Under Grants and Contracts with Hospitals," remain in effect.
- Appendix X, *Data Collection Form (Form SF-SAC)* – The Data Collection (Form SF-SAC) is available on the Federal Audit Clearinghouse (FAC) website.
- Appendix XI, *Compliance Supplement* – The *Compliance Supplement* is available on the OMB website.

Terminology

Nonfederal entity. A nonfederal entity means a state, local government, Indian tribe, institution of higher education, or nonprofit organization that carries out a federal award as a recipient or a subrecipient.

Must and should. The Uniform Guidance definitions of the terms *must* and *should* are different from those terms found in generally accepted auditing standards (GAAS) and generally accepted government auditing standards (GAGAS).

The Uniform Guidance uses the terms as follows:

- *Must* indicates a requirement in the document.
- *Should* indicates best practice or recommended approach. (*Should* does not indicate a requirement.)

Under GAAS and GAGAS, the term *must* indicates an unconditional requirement. GAAS and GAGAS define the term *should* as a presumptively mandatory requirement. An auditor must comply with a presumptively mandatory requirement in all cases in which such a requirement is relevant, except in rare cases as noted in that guidance.

Federal statutes versus laws. In the Uniform Guidance, the phrase "federal statutes, regulations, and the terms and conditions of federal awards" has replaced the phrase used in OMB Circular A-133: "laws, regulations, and the provisions of contracts or grant agreements." Note that variations of these terms are used in some cases.

Contractor versus vendor. The Uniform Guidance uses the term *contractor* instead of *vendor*. (However, the guidance relating to contractor versus subrecipient determination and characteristics of a payment to a contractor is substantially the same as that found in Circular A-133 relating to vendors.)

Equipment versus supplies. *Equipment* is defined as tangible personal property with a useful life of more than one year whose per-unit acquisition cost equals or exceeds $5,000 (or the capitalization threshold of the nonfederal entity if lower). *Supplies* are tangible personal property other than those described in equipment. Therefore, a computer or any computer-related device is a supply if it doesn't meet capitalization thresholds.

Knowledge check

1. Which is not a subpart within the Uniform Guidance?

    a. Subpart B – "General Provisions."
    b. Subpart D – "Post Federal Award Requirements."
    c. Subpart G – "Hospital Cost Principles."
    d. Subpart E – "Cost Principles."

2. What is the dollar threshold at which the Uniform Guidance requires a nonfederal entity to have a single audit?

    a. $300,000.
    b. $500,000.
    c. $750,000.
    d. $1,000,000.

Frequently asked questions

Frequently asked questions (FAQs) have been issued that provide clarifying information regarding specific sections of the Uniform Guidance. Periodically, FAQs are added to the document. As of February 2019, the last FAQs added were in July 2017. The FAQ document accumulates all FAQs and therefore includes all FAQs issued to date.

The FAQs are a great resource for clarifying certain key elements of the Uniform Guidance. For example, as part of the July 2017 update, FAQs were added regarding the following:

- Organizing content of the schedule of expenditures of federal awards (SEFA)
- Auditee responsibility for the summary schedule of prior audit findings and the corrective action plan
- Subtotals by agency in the SEFA

The FAQ are available https://cfo.gov/grants/uniform-guidance/.

Resources

GAQC

The GAQC is a voluntary membership center for CPA firms and state audit organizations designed to improve the quality and value of governmental audits. For the purposes of the GAQC, governmental audits are governmental audits include compliance audits (referred to as single audits) performed under the Single Audit Act Amendments of 1996 and the OMB Title 2 U.S. Code of Federal Regulations (CFR) Part 200, *Uniform Administrative Requirements, Cost Principles, and Audit Requirements for Federal Awards* (Uniform Guidance), program specific audits as defined under the Uniform Guidance, and other compliance audits and attestation engagements performed as required by federal, state, or local laws and regulations.

Governmental audits also include financial statement audits performed under *Government Auditing Standards* on entities such as states, local governments, not-for-profit organizations, institutions of higher education, and certain for-profit organizations.

The GAQC keeps members informed about the latest developments and provides them with tools and information to help them better manage their audit practice. Certain content on the GAQC's website referenced in this guide may be restricted to GAQC members only.

An Auditee Resource Center, open to the public, is also available on the GAQC website and provides information, practice aids, tools, and other resources that is of interest and benefit to auditees undergoing an audit performed under *Government Auditing Standards*.

For more information about the GAQC, visit the GAQC website at www.aicpa.org/gaqc.

AICPA resources

The AICPA has a number of different types of resources to assist recipients of federal awards and their auditors in understanding and implementing the reforms. Some of these resources are as follows:

- GAQC website (www.aicpa.org/gaqc)
- Self-study and group study courses
- Intermediate and advanced single audit certificates
- Periodic webcasts
- Audit Guide- *Government Auditing Standards* and Single Audits

Key point
The AICPA offers a new course — "The New Yellow Book: *Government Auditing Standards: 2018 Revision*," which covers everything you need to know about the new Yellow Book.

Single audit resources

AICPA	Summaries of recent auditing and other professional standards, as well as other AICPA activities.	www.aicpa.org www.aicpastore.com
Assistance Listings / Catalog of Federal Domestic Assistance (CFDA)	Electronic searchable version of the CFDA is available on beta.sam.gov which may be useful for identifying or verifying CFDA numbers.	https://beta.sam.gov/ (www.cfda.gov is now directed to the website noted here)
Department of Education: Office of Inspector General Nonfederal Audit Team	Provides sources, including various audit guides, to assist in the conduct and understanding of single audits and audits of student financial aid.	www2.ed.gov/about/offices/list/oig/nonfed/nfteam.html
Department of Health and Human Services (HHS): Office of Inspector General	Provides information regarding HHS agencies and their programs, including inspections of grant programs.	www.oig.hhs.gov
Department of Housing and Urban Development (HUD): Office of Inspector General	Among the items found on this website is the Consolidated Audit Guide for Audits of HUD Programs.	www.hudoig.gov
FAC	Website used for submission of data collection form. It is the repository of record for data collection forms and reporting packages.	https://harvester.census.gov/facweb/

GAO	Policy and guidance materials (including both the 2018 and 2011 Yellow Book) and reports on federal agency major rules.	www.gao.gov
GAQC	A membership center for firms and state audit organizations providing information and resources to those performing governmental audits.	www.aicpa.org/gaqc
U.S. Government Publishing Office	Includes a comprehensive list of available official federal resources (and related links) and is the official online bookstore for government publications.	www.gpo.gov/
IGnet	Includes electronic versions of the audit review guidelines that the federal inspectors general use in performing reviews of selected single audits.	www.ignet.gov/
OMB *Compliance Supplement*	The OMB *Compliance Supplement*, updated annually, is required to be used when performing a compliance audit under the Uniform Guidance.	The 2019 *Compliance Supplement* can be found at[1] https://www.whitehouse.gov/omb/management/office-federal-financial-management/

---

[1] As of the date this course was written, the 2020 *Compliance Supplement* was not yet issued.

Uniform Guidance — SEFA

The SEFA is a required part of the financial statements under the Uniform Guidance. Whereas the Uniform Guidance requires the auditor to determine whether the SEFA is fairly stated, in all material respects, in relation to the financial statements as a whole, the auditee is responsible for preparing the SEFA for the period covered by the auditee's financial statements.

The Uniform Guidance specifies the content required to be included in the SEFA. Because the SEFA serves as the primary basis for the auditor's major program determination, appropriate major program determination by the auditor is dependent on the accuracy and completeness of the information in the SEFA.

Under the Uniform Guidance, the auditee must prepare a SEFA that includes total federal awards expended. Items that are required to be placed on the face of the SEFA include the following:

- A list of individual federal programs by federal agency. For a cluster of programs, provide the cluster name, list individual federal programs within the cluster of programs, and provide the applicable federal agency name. For research and development (R&D), total federal awards expended must be shown either by individual federal award or by federal agency and major subdivision within the federal agency
- Total federal awards expended for each individual federal program and the CFDA number or other identification number (for a cluster of programs, the total for the cluster is also required)
- For federal awards received as a subrecipient, the name of the pass-through entity and identifying number assigned by the pass-through entity
- Total amount provided to subrecipients from each federal program
- Total amount of federal awards expended for loan or loan guarantee programs
- Noncash awards (for example, free rent, food commodities, donated property, and the value of insurance in effect)

The notes to the SEFA must include the following, at a minimum:

- A description of the significant accounting policies used in preparing the schedule
- The balances of loan and loan guarantee programs (loans) outstanding at the end of the audit period for those loans described in 2 CFR 200.502(b)
- *Whether or not* the auditee elected to use the 10% de minimus cost rate

Loans and loan guarantee programs. In determining the value of total federal awards expended for loan and loan guarantee programs, in addition to the value of new loans made or received during the audit period, auditees must include the balances of loans from previous years in the SEFA if the federal government imposes continuing compliance requirements. The Uniform Guidance does not define *continuing compliance requirement*. For loan or loan guarantee programs, identify in the notes to the schedule the balances outstanding at the end of the audit period. This is in addition to including the total federal awards expended for loan or loan guarantee programs in the schedule.

Subrecipients. If there are no subrecipients, a separate column for subrecipient amounts is not required. However, there is nothing to preclude an auditee from including such a column to indicate there were no amounts provided to subrecipients or, alternatively, an auditee could explain this in the notes to the SEFA (but this is not required).

The total amount of federal expenditures on the face of the SEFA will be the same as the total amount of federal expenditures for the data collection form. This same total typically will be the total used to calculate the type A threshold for determining major programs. (A final type A threshold calculation may be affected by the requirements in CFR 200.518(b)(3) for large loan and loan guarantee programs.)

No CFDA number

When no CFDA number is assigned or a CFDA number is not available, it is recommended that the auditee use the reporting format prescribed by the FAC in the SEFA. As noted in the instructions to Form SF-SAC, the required first two digits of the CFDA number identify the federal awarding agency. If the three-digit CFDA extension is unknown, the auditee will enter a "U" followed by a two-digit number. Therefore, the first federal program with an unknown three-digit extension would be "U01" for all award lines associated with that program, and the second would be "U02." For example, the number for the first HHS program with an unknown CFDA number would be 93.U01. The two-digit extension number can start over for each federal agency or continue through the reminder of the data collection form. If the program is part of the R&D cluster, then the instructions to Form SF-SAC state that "RD" is required as the CFDA extension (for example, 93.RD for an HHS program in the R&D cluster with an unknown CFDA extension). The FAC also requires that additional award identification be provided when the CFDA extension is unknown. This additional information used to identify the award may be the program year, contract number, or another such identifying number.

Common deficiencies found related to the preparation of the SEFA

A number of deficiencies related to the SEFA have been found over the past several years by the AICPA Professional Ethics Division and Peer Review Division as part of investigations of single audit engagements. A number of these deficiencies relate to the basic requirements for the SEFA, some of which are covered earlier.

1. The SEFA had missing information such as
    a. the CFDA number (or other identifying number when the CFDA information is not available),
    b. the name of the federal agency or the name of pass-through entity and identifying number assigned by the pass-through entity,
    c. the total federal expenditures for each federal program,
    d. total amounts provided to subrecipients,
    e. disclosure in the notes whether or not the auditee elected to use the 10% de minimus indirect cost rate, and
    f. notes describing the significant accounting policies used in preparing the schedule.

2. Improper clustering of programs or not clustering programs was found.
3. Lack of documentation related to the SEFA such as the following:
   a. Internal controls over preparation of the SEFA
   b. Procedures to determine whether the SEFA is fairly presented, in all material respects
   c. Appropriateness and completeness of the SEFA
   d. Reconciliation of the SEFA to amounts in the financial statements
4. Reporting, or referring to the reporting, on supplementary information and required supplementary information was not done.

Common deficiencies – SEFA

Take a look at the list of common deficiencies and consider doing a comparison to some of the SEFAs included in your single audits. This will assist you in identifying any missing pieces of the SEFAs that you audit.

Uniform Guidance — Determination of major programs

The process of identifying the major programs to audit is a four-step process.

The Uniform Guidance states that the auditor must use a risk-based approach to determine which federal programs are major programs. This risk-based approach must include consideration of current and prior audit experience, the oversight by federal agencies and pass-through entities, and the inherent risk of the federal program.

Step one — Determination of type A and type B programs

The auditor must identify the larger federal programs, which must be labeled type A programs. Type A programs are defined as federal programs with federal awards expended during the audit period exceeding the levels outlined in the following table.

Total federal awards expended[1]	Type A threshold
Equal to or exceed $750,000 but ≤ $25 million	$750,000
Exceed $25 million but ≤ $100 million	Total federal awards expended times 0.03
Exceed $100 million but ≤ $1 billion	$3 million
Exceed $1 billion but ≤ $10 billion	Total federal awards expended times 0.003
Exceed $10 billion but ≤ $20 billion	$30 million
Exceed $20 billion	Total federal awards expended times 0.0015

[1] Includes both cash and noncash awards.

Federal programs not labeled type A must be labeled type B programs.

For biennial audits the determination of type A and type B programs must be based upon the federal awards expended during the two-year period.

Large loan and loan guarantee programs in type A program determination

Under the Uniform Guidance, the inclusion of large loans and loan guarantee programs must not result in the exclusion of other programs as type A programs. The guidance regarding large loan and loan guarantee programs as it relates to the identification of the type A threshold is summarized as follows:

- For the purpose of this calculation, a program is considered to be a "federal program providing loans" if the value of federal awards expended for loans within the program comprises 50% or more of the total federal awards for the program. (**Note:** A cluster of programs is treated as one program.)
- When a *federal program providing loans* exceeds four times the largest nonloan program, it is considered a "large loan program," and the auditor must consider this federal program as a type A program and exclude its value in determining the type A threshold.
- The type A threshold is calculated after removing the total of all *large loan programs*.

Step two — Identification of low-risk type A programs

The auditor must identify type A programs that are low risk. In making the determination about whether a type A program is low risk, the auditor must consider whether there is an indication of significantly increased risk that would preclude the program from being low risk based on the following criteria:

- Oversight exercised by federal agencies and pass-through entities (for example, results of recent monitoring or other reviews or indication in the OMB *Compliance Supplement* that a federal agency has identified a federal program as higher risk)
- The results of audit follow-up
- Any changes in personnel or systems affecting the program that would indicate significantly increased risk that would preclude the program from being low risk

Key point
Note that these three criteria are the **only** criteria that the Uniform Guidance permits the auditor to consider in evaluating whether there is significantly increased risk for a type A program (that is, the auditor is not permitted to use judgment based on the inherent risk of a type A program).

In addition, for a type A program to be considered low risk, it must

- have been audited as a major program in at least one of the two most recent audit periods, and
- not have had any of the following in the most recent audit period:
  - Internal control deficiencies, which were identified as material weaknesses in the auditor's report on internal control for major programs
  - A modified opinion on the program in the auditor's report on major programs
  - Known or likely questioned costs that exceed 5% of the total federal awards expended for the program

The Uniform Guidance permits a federal awarding agency to request that a type A program for certain recipients not be considered low risk so that it would be audited as a major program.

Key point
If no low-risk type A programs are identified in step 2, the auditor skips step 3 and moves directly to step 4.

Step three — Identification of high-risk type B programs

The auditor must identify type B programs that are high risk using professional judgment and the following criteria from section 200.519, *Criteria for Federal Program Risk*:

- Current and prior audit experience
- Oversight exercised by federal agencies and pass-through entities
- Inherent risk of noncompliance of the federal programs

However, the auditor is not required to identify more high-risk type B programs than at least one-fourth the number of type A programs identified as low risk under step 2. Once this number of high-risk type B programs have been identified (that is, at least one-fourth the number of low-risk type A programs), the auditor can discontinue further risk assessments of type B programs.

The Uniform Guidance does not require a specific number of high-risk type B programs to be identified. It is possible to risk assess all of an auditee's type B programs and determine that fewer than one-quarter the number of low-risk type A programs are high-risk type B programs, or that none are high-risk type B programs.

Key point
Under the Uniform Guidance, all type B programs **identified** as high risk are required to be audited as major programs. To the extent that an auditor performs risk assessments on type B programs beyond what is required and identifies more high-risk type B programs than required (that is, at least one-fourth the number of low-risk type A programs), those additional high-risk type B programs **must** be audited as major programs.

Except for known material weaknesses in internal control or compliance problems, a single criterion in risk would seldom cause a type B program to be considered high risk. When determining which type B programs to risk assess, the auditor is encouraged to use an approach that provides an opportunity for different high-risk type B programs to be audited as major over a period of time.

Key point
The auditor is not expected to perform risk assessments on relatively small federal programs. The auditor is required only to perform risk assessments on type B programs that exceed 25% (0.25) of the type A threshold as determined in step 1.

Step four — Selection of programs to be audited as major

At a minimum, the auditor must audit all the following as major programs:

- All type A programs not identified as low risk under step 2
- All type B programs identified as high risk under step 3
- Programs to be audited as major based on a federal agency or pass-through entity request
- Additional programs as necessary to meet the percentage of coverage requirements

Key point
If preliminary numbers were initially used or any adjustments are made to total federal expenditures during the audit, the major program determination should be reperformed to be sure that the correct major programs were selected for testing.
Use final numbers!

Percentage of coverage rule

If the auditee meets the criteria for a low-risk auditee, the auditor needs to audit only major programs that, in aggregate, encompass at least 20% (0.20) of total federal awards expended. Otherwise, the auditor must audit the major programs that, in aggregate, encompass at least 40% (0.40) of total federal awards expended.

Low-risk auditee requirements

An auditee that meets all the following conditions for each of the preceding two audit periods qualifies as a low-risk auditee and is eligible for reduced audit coverage:

- The entity must have had single audits performed on an annual basis. A nonfederal entity that has biennial audits does not qualify as a low-risk auditee.
- The entity must have submitted the data collection form and reporting package to the FAC on time.
- The auditor's opinion on whether the entity's financial statements were prepared in accordance with generally accepted accounting principles (GAAP) or a basis of accounting required by state law and the auditor's in-relation-to opinion on the SEFA were unmodified. Therefore, unless required by state law, an auditee that prepares its financial statements on a non-GAAP basis of accounting, such as the cash or modified cash basis, cannot be considered a low-risk auditee.
- The entity had no deficiencies in internal control that were identified as material weaknesses under the Yellow Book.
- The auditor did not report a substantial doubt about the entity's ability to continue as a going concern.
- None of the entity's federal programs had audit findings from any of the following in either of the preceding two audit periods in which they were classified as type A programs:
  - Internal control deficiencies that were identified as material weaknesses in the auditor's report on internal control for major programs
  - A modified opinion on a major program in the auditor's report on major programs
  - Known or likely questioned costs that exceeded 5% of the total federal awards expended for a type A program during the audit period

Note: There is no provision in the Uniform Guidance that allows a cognizant or oversight agency to provide a waiver of the low-risk auditee criteria.

Common deficiencies related to major program determination

The following are common deficiencies related to the major program determination found over the past several years by the AICPA Professional Ethics Division and Peer Review Division as part of investigations of single audit engagements:

1. The auditor failed to accurately identify or test (or both) all major programs in accordance with the requirements. The most common reasons found are as follows:
   a. Using preliminary expenditures when the final expenditures resulted in a program being an other than low risk program
   b. Failure to properly perform type A and type B program risk assessments
   c. Failure to combine expenditures from various funding agents having the same CFDA number
   d. Improper clustering of related program CFDA numbers
   e. Using an improper threshold
   f. Failure to consider large loans in the major program threshold assessment
2. The auditor improperly identified the entity as a low-risk auditee which resulted in insufficient coverage. The most common reasons found are the following:
   a. The auditee did not file a data collection form in a prior year
   b. A modified opinion was issued within the prior two years, either over the financial statements or the SEFA
   c. There were material weaknesses in internal controls over financial reporting or federal compliance within the last two years
   d. There was material noncompliance in federal programs within the last two years

---

Knowledge check

3. What is a large loan program?

   a. A federal program providing loans that exceeds two times the largest nonloan program.
   b. A federal program providing loans that exceeds three times the largest nonloan program.
   c. A federal program providing loans that exceeds four times the largest nonloan program.
   d. A federal program providing loans that exceeds five times the largest nonloan program.

4. As it relates to using professional judgment in the determination of major programs, which statement is correct?

   a. Type A programs allow for more professional judgment than type B programs.
   b. Type A programs allow for less professional judgment than type B programs.
   c. Type A programs allow for the same amount of professional judgment than type B programs.
   d. Professional judgment is not permitted in major program determination.

5. An auditor is not required to perform risk assessments on relatively small type B programs. Under the Uniform Guidance, an auditor is required to perform risk assessments on type B programs exceeding what amount?

    a. $100,000.
    b. $50,000.
    c. 25% of the type A threshold.
    d. 20% of the type A threshold.

Uniform Guidance – Reporting considerations

There are many aspects to reporting in a single audit. The topics discussed subsequently are only some of the many related to reporting in a single audit.

Audit findings

Audit findings reported

Under the Uniform Guidance, the auditor must report the following as audit findings in a schedule of findings and questioned costs:

- Significant deficiencies and material weaknesses in internal control over major programs
- Material noncompliance with the provisions of federal statutes, regulations, or the terms and conditions of federal awards related to a major program
- Known questioned costs that are greater than $25,000 for a type of compliance requirement for a major program
- Known questioned costs when likely questioned costs are greater than $25,000 for a type of compliance requirement for a major program
- Known questioned costs that are greater than $25,000 for a federal program that is not audited as a major program
- The circumstances concerning why the auditor's report on compliance for each major program is other than an unmodified opinion, unless such circumstances are otherwise reported as audit findings in the schedule of findings and questioned costs
- Known or likely fraud affecting a federal award, unless such fraud is otherwise reported as an audit finding in the schedule of findings and questioned costs
- Significant instances of abuse relating to major programs
- Instances where the results of audit follow-up procedures disclosed that the summary schedule of prior audit findings, prepared by the auditee, materially misrepresents the status of any prior audit finding

Audit findings detail

The required audit findings must include the following specific information, as applicable:

- Federal program and specific federal award identification including
  - the CFDA title and number,
  - federal award identification number and year, name of federal agency, and
  - name of the applicable pass-through entity.
- The criteria or specific requirement upon which the audit finding is based, including the federal statutes, regulations, or the terms and conditions of the federal awards.

- The condition found, including facts that support the deficiency identified in the audit finding.
- A statement of cause that identifies the reason or explanation for the condition or the factors responsible for the difference between the situation that exists (condition) and the required or desired state (criteria), which may also serve as a basis for recommendations for corrective action.
- The possible asserted effect to provide sufficient information to the auditee and federal agency or pass-through entity (in the case of a subrecipient) to permit them to determine the cause and effect to facilitate prompt and proper corrective action.
- Identification of questioned costs and how they were computed. Known questioned costs must be identified by applicable CFDA number(s) and applicable federal award identification number(s).
- Information to provide proper perspective for judging the prevalence and consequences of the audit findings, such as whether the audit findings represent an isolated instance or a systemic problem. Where appropriate, instances identified must be related to the universe and the number of cases examined and must be quantified in terms of dollar value. The auditor should report whether the sampling was a statistically valid sample.
- Identification of whether the audit finding was a repeat of a finding in the immediately prior audit and, if so, any applicable prior year audit finding numbers.
  Note: If you had a finding in the prior year (i.e. 2017-002) and this year it is a repeat finding, when you number your finding for the current year, it should be finding 2018-00X; and then, in the details, it should indicate the prior year finding number of 2017-002.
- Recommendations to prevent future occurrences of the deficiency identified in the audit finding.
- Views of responsible officials of the auditee (not only when there is disagreement with the audit finding).
- A reference number in the format meeting the requirements of the data collection form submission to allow for easy referencing of the audit findings during follow-up.

Audit finding detail in a single audit should also meet the presentation requirements of *Government Auditing Standards*.

Auditee responsibilities

Corrective action plan

At the end of the audit, the auditee must prepare a corrective action plan to address each audit finding included in the current year auditor's report. This includes findings relating to the financial statements required to be reported in accordance with GAGAS. The corrective action plan must provide

- the name(s) of the contact person(s) responsible for corrective action,
- the corrective action planned for each audit finding (referred to by the auditor-assigned reference number), and
- the anticipated completion date.

If the auditee does not agree with the audit findings, or believes corrective action is not required, the corrective action plan must contain an explanation and specific reasons why the auditee disagrees.

The corrective action plan is required to be prepared by the auditee and placed on auditee letterhead, as clarified in FAQ 511-1. FAQ 511-1 also states that the auditee may not simply reference the views of responsible officials' section of the findings to fulfill its responsibility for the preparation of a corrective action plan. It also states that the auditor should not prepare the corrective action plan or summary schedule of prior audit findings for the auditee. The 2017 FAQ document can be found at https://cfo.gov//wp-content/uploads/2017/08/July2017-UniformGuidanceFrequently AskedQuestions.pdf.

Summary schedule of prior audit findings

The Uniform Guidance requires the auditee to prepare a summary schedule of prior audit findings when audit findings were not corrected or were only partially corrected. The summary schedule must describe the reasons for the finding's recurrence and planned corrective action, and any partial corrective action taken. The summary schedule of prior audit findings must include findings relating to the financial statements, which are required to be reported in accordance with *Government Auditing Standards*. Although FAQ 511-1 does not specifically extend the requirement regarding letterhead to the summary schedule of prior audit findings, requesting that the auditee's summary schedule of prior audit findings be placed on auditee letterhead would be consistent with FAQ question 511-1 and would more clearly delineate the schedule as auditee-prepared information.

FAC — Data collection form

All federal agencies, pass-through entities, and others interested in a reporting package and data collection form must obtain it by accessing the FAC.

Key point
The data collection form is updated every three years. A revised form and related instructions were released in June 2019. The new form is effective for fiscal period ending dates in 2019, 2020, and 2021 and should not be used for audits prior to these dates.

FAC

The FAC must make the reporting packages received available to the public (except for Indian tribes exercising the option described in the following section), maintain a database of completed audits, provide appropriate information to federal agencies, and follow up with known auditees that have not submitted the required data collection forms and reporting packages.

Key updates

Following are the key changes included in the final form and the updates made to the Internet Data Entry System (IDES):

- Auditees will now have the option to generate a customizable schedule of expenditures of federal awards and related notes to the SEFA from IDES that could be included in the reporting package. Auditees will also be able to enter the federal award information and notes to the SEFA prior to the fiscal period end date and the audit work being conducted.
- IDES will now include an auditee Employer Identification Number edit check.
- Auditees will be required to transfer the text of the notes to the SEFA and their corrective action plans (CAPs) into the form.
- Auditors will be required to transfer the text of audit findings into the form.
- IDES will offer an optional worksheet-type function to assist in the transferring of text from audit findings and CAPs using an Excel template document that will be able to be downloaded, completed, and then uploaded.
- With regard to all text transferred into the form by both auditees and auditors, the system will not allow for the transfer of charts and tables embedded within the original documents. Instead, preparers will have to include a notation within transferred text referring readers to the actual underlying note, CAP, or finding for relevant charts and tables.
- When a previous FAC submission is revised and resubmitted to the FAC, auditees will be required to indicate in IDES what has changed and the reason why. This information will also be part of the public database.

Exception for Indian tribes

An auditee that is an Indian tribe may opt not to authorize the FAC to make the reporting package publicly available on a website, by excluding the authorization for the FAC publication in the statement described previously. If this option is exercised, the auditee becomes responsible for submitting the reporting package directly to any pass-through entities through which it has received a federal award and to pass-through entities for which the summary schedule of prior audit findings reported the status of any findings related to federal awards that the pass-through entity provided. Unless restricted by federal statute or regulation, if the auditee opts not to authorize publication, it must make copies of the reporting package available for public inspection.

Common deficiencies related to auditor reporting in a single audit

The following are common deficiencies related to reporting in a single audit found over the past several years by the AICPA Professional Ethics Division and Peer Review Division as part of investigations of single audit engagements. Note that some of the investigations were for audit periods required to be audited under Circular A-133, however, the issues listed are still valid for an audit performed under the Uniform Guidance. Deficiencies found included the following:

- Financial statement report. Failure to include all of the required elements of professional standards in the Independent Auditor's Report, including the following omissions:
  - Reference to the engagement being performed in accordance with *Government Auditing Standards*

- Identification of the governmental entity's major funds and opinion units presented
- Addressing supplemental information and required supplemental information
- Reference to prior year financial statements when comparative years are presented
- Reference to the internal control report issued under *Government Auditing Standards*

- Yellow Book report. Failure to include all of the required elements of professional standards in the Auditor's Report on Internal Control over Financial Reporting and on Compliance and Other Matters, including omitting
  - "Independent" from report title,
  - a reference, or an incorrect reference, to material weaknesses or significant deficiencies included in the Schedule of Findings and Questioned Costs — indicating that there were no significant deficiencies identified,
  - a clause stating that the entity's responses were not audited and that the auditor expresses no opinion on those responses, and
  - a purpose alert.
- The auditor did not properly date the audit report. This usually occurred because the auditor reissued the report as a result of additional disclosures or audit procedures but did not dual-date or re-date the report. However, there have also been instances in which the auditor dated the report before obtaining sufficient evidence.
- The auditor's report did not contain an appropriate indication of the character of the examination and the degree of responsibility taken with respect to the required supplementary information or supplementary information accompanying the basic financial statements other than with respect to the SEFA.
- Auditors did not comply with AU-C section 265, *Communicating Internal Control Related Matters Identified in an Audit* (AICPA *Professional Standards*), in wording their reports. The definitions of control deficiencies, significant deficiencies, and material weaknesses followed language in superseded guidance.
- The auditor's report on internal control over financial reporting and on compliance and other matters based on an audit of financial statements performed in accordance with *Government Auditing Standards* failed to describe the auditor's departure from the standard unmodified opinion on the financial statements.
- The auditor did not report audit findings in the schedule of findings and questioned costs with
  - all of the required elements,
  - the specific federal award identification including CFDA number,
  - the name of the federal agency,
  - the reference number or any other required component of a finding, or
  - a combination of any of these items.
- Failure to properly and consistently report the results of the single audit between the auditor's reports, the schedule of findings and questioned costs, and the data collection form, including major program determination and threshold, low-risk auditee status, and evaluation of findings.
- Failure to undergo a peer review as required by state board Yellow Book requirements (or both) or by the requirements of the AICPA or state CPA society (or both).
- Failure to submit timely the data collection form to the FAC for the current year audit.
- Improper reference to Circular A-133, and not the Uniform Guidance, the auditor's reporting.

Knowledge check

6. Which statement is accurate regarding the corrective action plan?

    a. The corrective action plan is the same document as the schedule of finding and questioned cost.

    b. The corrective action plan must be prepared by the auditee.

    c. The corrective action plan must be prepared by the auditor on auditor letterhead.

    d. The corrective action plan is optional.

Protected personally identifiable information

Auditees and auditors must ensure that their respective parts of the reporting package do not include protected personally identifiable information, or PPII. PPII is information that can be used to distinguish or trace an individual's identity, either alone or when combined with other personal or identifying information that is linked or linkable to a specific individual. Some information that is considered to be PPII is available in public sources such as telephone books, public websites, and university listings. This type of information is considered to be *public PPII* and includes, for example, first and last name, address, work telephone number, email address, home telephone number, and general educational credentials. The definition of PPII is not anchored to any single category of information or technology. Rather, it requires a case-by-case assessment of the specific risk that an individual can be identified. Non-PPII can become PPII whenever additional information is made publicly available, in any medium and from any source, that, when combined with other available information, could be used to identify an individual.

PPII is defined in the Uniform Guidance as "an individual's first name or first initial and last name in combination with any one or more of types of information, including, but not limited to, Social Security number, passport number, credit card numbers, clearances, bank numbers, biometrics, date and place of birth, mother's maiden name, criminal, medical, and financial records, and educational transcripts. This does not include PII that is required by law to be disclosed."

Uniform Guidance — Procurement standards

After a three-year grace period for adopting the Uniform Guidance procurement standards, all entities are now subject to the Uniform Guidance procurement standards. The information here sets forth a summary of some of the provisions.

When states make property and services purchases, they must follow the same policies and procedures used for procurements from its nonfederal funds. All other nonfederal entities (including subrecipients of a state) must use its own documented procedures which reflect the Uniform Guidance requirements. The requirements include additional documentation regarding conflicts of interest including organizational conflict of interest policies. Nonfederal entities must oversee contractors, avoid acquisition of unnecessary or duplicative items, use only responsible contractors, and maintain sufficient records.

Nonfederal entities must maintain records sufficient to detail the history of procurement. The Uniform Guidance has specific documentation requirements regarding procurement. Entities must document

- rationale for the method of procurement,
- selection of contract type,
- contractor selection or rejection, and
- basis for the contract price.

Permitted methods of procurement

Nonfederal entities must use one of the following methods of procurement:

- Procurement by micro-purchases. Micro-purchases must be distributed equitably among qualified suppliers.
- Procurement by small purchase procedures (those less than the simplified acquisition threshold). Quotations must be obtained from an adequate number of qualified sources. Adequate number is not defined in the guidance.
- Procurement by sealed bids (preferred method for construction contracts) submitted in response to formal advertising[2] and providing sufficient response time prior to the bid opening date. Fixed-price contracts are awarded to lowest bidder.
- Competitive proposal. Request for proposal must be publicized with proposals solicited from an adequate number of qualified sources. The entity must have a written method for conducting evaluations of proposals received. The contract must be awarded to the firm with a proposal most advantageous to the program — price and other factors considered.
- Noncompetitive proposals are appropriate ONLY when
  - goods or services are available only from a single source,
  - there is a public emergency,
  - after soliciting a number of sources competition is deemed inadequate, and
  - the awarding agency expressly authorized noncompetitive proposals in response to a written request from organization.

---

[2] Only local and tribal governments are required to publicly advertise the invitation to bid and to open bids publicly.

A nonfederal entity must perform a cost or price analysis for every procurement action in excess of the simplified acquisition threshold, including contract modifications. In addition, an independent estimate of the cost must be made before receiving bids or proposals.

> **Note:** Auditors and nonfederal entities need to pay particular attention to the growing number of exceptions. There have been exceptions made to thresholds (like the micro-purchase threshold) for several agencies. Confirming with the agency is the easiest way to ensure proper compliance.

Knowledge check

7. Which is **not** an approved method of procurement?

   a. Procurement by macro-purchases.
   b. Procurement by small purchase procedures.
   c. Procurement by sealed bid.
   d. Noncompetitive proposal.

Cost principles in a single audit

The Uniform Guidance consolidates the cost principles (other than those related to hospitals) into a single document with limited variations by type of entity. The guidance consolidated the requirements from OMB Circulars A-21, A-87, A-89, A-102, A-110, A-122, and the guidance in Circular A-50 on Single Audit Act follow-up.

Appendix IX, "Hospital Cost Principles," of the Uniform Guidance notes that the cost principles applicable to hospitals are not superseded with the issuance of the Uniform Guidance. Until revised guidance is implemented for hospitals, the existing principles at 45 CFR Part 75 Appendix IX, "Principles for Determining Costs Applicable to Research and Development Under Grants and Contracts with Hospitals," remain in effect.

Key point
Although hospital cost principles are not superseded by the Uniform Guidance, hospitals are required to comply with the requirements of the Uniform Guidance other than the cost principles.

Nonfederal entities

The Uniform Guidance defines a nonfederal entity as a "state, local government, Indian tribe, institution of higher education, or not-for-profit (NFP) organization that carries out a federal award as a recipient or subrecipient." (The Uniform Guidance does not apply to for-profit organizations.) Nonfederal entities are required to implement the Uniform Guidance administrative requirements and cost principles for all new federal awards and to certain funding increments made on or after December 26, 2014. As it relates to funding increments, note the following:

- For awards made before December 26, 2014, funding increments issued on or after December 26, 2014, where the agency *modified the terms and conditions of the award*, are subject to the Uniform Guidance administrative requirements and cost principles.
- For awards made before December 26, 2014, funding increments issued on or after December 26, 2014, *with no changes to the award terms and conditions,* continue to be subject to the applicable pre-Uniform Guidance requirements.

The effective date of the Uniform Guidance as it relates to a subaward is the same as the effective date of the federal award from which the subaward is made.

Impact of the effective date of the administrative requirements and cost principles

What does this mean to the auditee?

Nonfederal entities may have some awards subject to the pre-Uniform Guidance circulars and other federal awards subject to the Uniform Guidance administrative requirements and cost principles. This may be the case within a single major program that is funded through multiple funding sources.

What does this mean to the auditor?

In light of the Uniform Guidance effective date provisions, as part of the audit planning process, auditors should determine the applicable criteria that are required to be used in performing the compliance audit for an award (that is, whether an award is subject to pre-Uniform Guidance administrative requirements and cost principles circulars versus the Uniform Guidance requirements). Federal awarding documents will be important tools for making this determination. Nonfederal entities and auditors with questions regarding the applicable criteria for federal awards may consult with agency single audit coordinators or program officials. Contact information for these agency representatives can be found in Appendix III, "Federal Agency Single Audit, Key Management Liason, and Program Contacts" of the *Compliance Supplement*.

Key point
This situation may occur within a major program when the major program is funded through multiple funding sources.

When a nonfederal entity has both federal awards subject to the pre-Uniform Guidance requirements and the Uniform Guidance administrative requirements and cost principles, compliance testing will test against either the pre-Uniform Guidance criteria or the Uniform Guidance criteria depending on federal award dates. A separate sample for transactions subject to the pre-Uniform Guidance requirements and those subject to the Uniform Guidance requirements within a major program would not typically be needed when performing tests of compliance. However, it is recommended that the documentation include an identification of which set of guidance a transaction is subject to.

Key point
Having an audit performed under the Uniform Guidance audit requirements has no impact on the effective date provisions of the Uniform Guidance administrative requirements and cost principles. Furthermore, having federal awards subject to pre-Uniform Guidance administrative requirements and cost principles has no effect on the audit requirements used. All audits are performed under the Uniform Guidance.

Note: There is a separate section of the *Compliance Supplement* for auditing federal awards that are subject to the circulars that existed prior to the Uniform Guidance (Part 3.1) and a separate section for those that are subject to the Uniform Guidance (part 3.2). The audit steps can be different between part 3.1 and part 3.2. For example, for the "allowability" compliance requirements, the underlying cost principles and administrative requirements that are referred to in parts 3.1 and 3.2 are different.

Federal cost principles

The Uniform Guidance cost principles guidance includes the following topics:

- General provisions
- Basic considerations
  - For example, allowability, allocable costs, and prior written approval
- Direct and indirect costs
  - Direct costs can be identified specifically with a particular final cost objective (for example, a federal award)
  - Indirect costs must be classified in either the "facilities" or "administration" category
- Special considerations for states, local governments, and Indian tribes
- Special considerations for institutions of higher education
- General provision for selected items of cost
  - Includes a number of specific types of costs

Key point
Direct costs are defined as those that can be specifically identified with a particular cost objective such as a federal award or that can be directly assigned to such activities relatively easily with a high degree of accuracy. The Uniform Guidance states that the identification of a cost with a federal award (rather than the nature of the goods or services received) is the determining factor in distinguishing between direct and indirect costs.

Some of the more significant requirements relating to the federal cost principles follow.

- Indirect cost rates
  - Most nonfederal entities that have never received a negotiated indirect cost rate may elect to charge a *de minimis* rate of 10% of modified total direct costs, which may be used indefinitely.
  - Any nonfederal entity that has a federally negotiated indirect cost rate may apply for a one-time extension of a current negotiated indirect cost rate for a period of up to four years.
- Required certifications
  - Annual and final fiscal reports (or vouchers) requesting payment signed by an official who is authorized to legally bind the nonfederal entity. The required language for this certification is located in section 200.415, *Required Certifications*.
  - Cost allocation plan or indirect cost rate proposal.

- For NFP entities only, certifications as appropriate that they did not meet the definition of a major corporation as defined in section 200.414, *Indirect (F&A) Costs*.
- Collection costs incurred to recover improper payments are allowable as direct or indirect costs.
- Conference costs incurred by a sponsor or host may include the costs of identifying (not providing) locally available dependent care resources. Additionally, temporary dependent care costs, above and beyond regular dependent care resulting directly from travel to conferences, are allowable under certain circumstances.
- Standards for documentation of personnel expenses include the following:
  - Charges to federal awards must be based on records that accurately reflect the work performed. Such records must
    - be supported by a system of internal control that provides reasonable assurance the charges are accurate, allowable, and properly allocated;
    - be incorporated into the official records of the nonfederal entity;
    - reasonably reflect the total activity for which the employee is compensated;
    - encompass both federally assisted and all other activities compensated by the nonfederal entity on an integrated basis;
    - comply with established accounting policies and practices of the nonfederal entity; and
    - support the distribution of the employee's salary or wages among specific activities or federal award or other cost objective (for employees working on more than one federal award, a federal award and a nonfederal award, an indirect cost activity and a direct cost activity, and other similar circumstances).
    - Nonfederal entities meeting the previously noted standards will not be required to provide additional support or documentation for the work performed other than that required under U.S. Department of Labor regulations implementing the Fair Labor Standards Act of 1938.
  - Charges for salaries and wages of nonexempt employees must be supported by records indicating the total number of hours worked each day in addition to the previously noted documentation requirements.
    - In certain circumstances, states, local governments, and Indian tribes, may use substitute processes or systems for allocating salaries and wages to federal awards in place of or in addition to the requirements noted previously.
    - When records of a nonfederal entity do not meet the standards prescribed, the federal government may require personnel activity reports including prescribed certifications or equivalent documentation to support the records required in the cost principles.

In addition to the requirements in subpart E, specific guidance relating to indirect costs, indirect cost proposals, and central service cost allocation plans is provided in the following appendixes to the Uniform Guidance.

Appendix III to Part 200	*Indirect (F&A) Costs Identification and Assignment, and Rate Determination for Institutions of Higher Education (IHEs)*
Appendix IV to Part 200	Indirect (F&A) Costs Identification and Assignment, and Rate Determination for Nonprofit Organizations

Appendix V to Part 200	*State/Local Government-wide Central Service Cost Allocation Plans*
Appendix VI to Part 200	*Public Assistance Cost Allocation Plans*
Appendix VII to Part 200	*States and Local Government and Indian Tribe Indirect Cost Proposals*

Knowledge check

8. Which statement is correct regarding cost principles?

    a. Uniform Guidance cost principles includes a section on hospital cost principles.
    b. All nonfederal entities are required to use the Uniform Guidance cost principles for all federal awards.
    c. Uniform Guidance cost principles apply to for-profit entities that expend federal awards received directly from a federal agency.
    d. The identification of a cost with a federal award determines whether it is a direct or indirect cost.

Government-wide audit quality study

The Uniform Guidance provides for a government-wide audit quality project to be performed every six years beginning in 2018. The results of this study must be made public. The stated purpose of this project is to determine the quality of single audits by providing a statistically reliable estimate of the extent that single audits conform to applicable requirements, standards, and procedures and to make recommendations to address noted audit quality issues, which may include changes to the requirements.

FAQ 200.513 indicates that the quality study will examine single audit engagements that are submitted to the FAC no earlier than 2018, as determined by OMB. There has been no more recent information regarding the timing of the study than this.

Now is the time to prepare!

Proposed changes to the Uniform Guidance

In January 2020, the OMB issued proposed changes to the Uniform Guidance. Part 200.109 requires review every five years, so the proposal was not unexpected. The focus of the changes was in three main areas — implementation of the President's Management Agenda (PMA), Results-Oriented Accountability for Grants Cross-Agency Priority Goal, alignment with other authoritative sources, and clarification of existing requirements. As part of the alignment with the Cross-Agency Priority goals, it has been noted that grants managers report spending a disproportionate amount of time using antiquated processes to monitor compliance. The PMA was designed to move the grants area to focus on modernization to allow grants managers to shift their time to analyzing data to improve results. This can be seen in several areas of the changes.

The PMA had four key strategies:

- Standardize the Grants Management Business Process and Data
  - Changing terminology to be consistent between 2 CFR and Grants Management Federal Integrated Business Framework
  - Standardizing data elements
- Build Shared IT Infrastructure
- Manage Risk
- Achieve Program Goals & Objectives

Several new regulations need to be incorporated into the Uniform Guidance including several NDAA, Federal Funding Accountability and Transparency Act (FFATA), Digital Accountability and Transparency Act (DATA Act) and Never Contract with the Enemy

These are larger proposed changes:

- Micro-purchase threshold
  - Incorporates the guidance in M-18-18
  - $10,000 for all recipients
  - Proposes to extend flexibility to request a higher micro-purchase threshold to all nonfederal entities
- Merit Reviews
  - Extends merit review process to all awards in which the Federal awarding agency has the discretion to choose the recipient
  - Clarifies that the objective is to select recipients most likely to be successful in delivering results
- Domestic Preferencees
  - Executive Order 13788, Buy American and Hire American
  - Executive Order 13858, Strengthening Buy American Preferences for Infrastructure Projects
    - Encouraged to the extent permitted by law to maximize use of materials produced in the United States
- Standardize Terminology
  - Update definition of period of performance
  - Replace term obligation with either financial obligation or responsibility to align with the DATA Act
  - Replace CFDA with Assistance listing number
  - Clarify that a management decision is a written determination
  - Replace standard form with common form

- Does not have to be all agencies
- Encourage efficiency and collaboration
  - Reformatting Subpart A to remove section numbers
    - Facilitate future edits
- Program Planning and Design
  - New section emphasizes the importance of focusing on performance to achieve results
    - Focus on the balance between performance and compliance
    - Results-oriented grants
    - Focus on program design by establishing goals, objectives, and indicators
    - Require agencies to provide recipients with clear performance goals, indicators and milestones
  - Encourages requests for exceptions to be innovative and apply a risk-based, data-driven framework
    - Focus on performance
  - Foundations of Evidence-Based Policymaking Act of 2018
    - Emphasizes collaboration and coordination
- Terminology Changes
  - Updates definition of termination to strengthen the ability of the agency to terminate awards, to greatest extent authorized by law, when the award no longer effectuates the program goals or agency priorities
    - Prioritize support to awards that meet program goals
- Fixed Amount Awards
  - Expands to both grant agreements and cooperative agreements
- Program Evaluation Costs
  - Emphasizes evaluation costs are allowed as a direct cost
- Non-authoritative Guidance
  - Prohibits agencies from including references to non-authoritative guidance in the terms and conditions
- Machine-readable formats
  - Reinforces the machine-readable requirements support the Leveraging Data as a Strategic Asset Cross-Agency Priority goal
- Grant Oversight and New Efficiency (GONE) Act
  - Increase the number of days to submit closeout reports and to liquidate all financial obligations from 90 days to 120 days for pass-through entities
    - No changes to subrecipients
- Audit Quality Project
  - Shifts the data from 2018 to 2021
- Expanded De Minimus Rate
  - Allows the use of 10% de minimus rate for all non-federal entities with exceptions
  - Clarifies that the non-federal entity is not required to provide proof of costs that are covered under that rate
- Negotiated Rates
  - Requires all grantees with negotiated agreements for indirect costs rates to collect and display the agreements on a public website
    - The agency that will be responsible and the website that will be used will be designated by OMB
    - The goal is transparency

- NDAA 2019
  - Addresses prohibited telecommunication and video surveillance services or equipment
  - Focuses on foreign entities
- Never Contract with the Enemy
  - Requires agencies to utilize the System for Award Management Exclusions and the Federal Awardee Performance and Integrity Information System to ensure compliance before awarding a grant or cooperative agreement
- FFATA
  - Clarifies that federal agencies may receive federal financial assistance
  - Increases transparency of awards received by federal agencies
- GASB 68
  - Revises Compensation section to claim pension costs that are actual and funded
- Questioned Costs
  - Clarifies questioned costs are not improper payments until reviewed and confirmed to be improper
- Pass-Through Entities (PTE)
  - Clarifies PTEs are only responsible for follow up on findings related to their subaward
- FAQs
  - Incorporates priors FAQs that were issued separately into the Uniform Guidance

Common deficiencies found in single audits

The AICPA accumulates information regarding common deficiencies found in single audits that have been identified in ethics investigations and peer reviews. The deficiencies relate to nearly all areas of a single audit. Some common deficiencies are provided here as they relate to the following areas of a single audit:

- Planning the single audit
- Internal control over compliance
- Sampling
- Audit of compliance
- Preparation of the SEFA
- Major program determination
- Single audit reporting

Deficiencies identified related to the preparation of the SEFA, major program determination, and single audit reporting were previously discussed in this course.

Planning the single audit

In a single audit, there are a number of additional considerations in planning the audit. One of these is making sure the additional audit requirements are identified while gaining an understanding of how GAAS and *Government Auditing Standards* affect the compliance audit. Adequate planning assists in gaining audit efficiency and helps to ensure that the audit is performed in accordance with professional standards.

The following are common deficiencies related to planning the single audit that have been found over the past several years by the AICPA Professional Ethics Division and Peer Review Division as part of investigations of single audit engagements:

- Failure to properly document independence considerations required by the Yellow Book including the evaluation of management's skill, knowledge, and experience to effectively oversee nonaudit services performed by the auditor, evaluation of significant threats, and safeguards applied to reduce threats to an acceptable level
- Failure to meet the Yellow Book CPE requirements including 80 hours of A&A and 24 hours of CPE that directly relate to government auditing, the government environment, or the specific or unique environment in which the auditee operates
- Lack of documentation of the risk of material noncompliance for the major program's compliance requirements occurring due to fraud

Internal control over compliance

The requirements related to internal control in a single audit are beyond those of a financial statement audit conducted in accordance with GAAS and GAGAS.

As it relates to internal control, in addition to the requirements of GAAS and GAGAS, the Uniform Guidance states that the auditor must

- perform procedures to obtain an understanding of internal control over federal programs sufficient to plan the audit to support a low assessed level of control risk of noncompliance for major programs,
- plan the testing of internal control over compliance for major programs to support a low assessed level of control risk of noncompliance for the assertions relevant to the compliance requirements for each major program,
- perform testing of internal control over compliance as planned, and
- report on internal control over compliance describing the scope of testing of internal control and the results of the tests and, where applicable, refer to the separate schedule of findings and questioned costs.

With this in mind, the following are common deficiencies related to internal control over compliance found over the past several years by the AICPA Professional Ethics Division and Peer Review Division as part of investigations of single audit engagements:

- Failure to document an understanding of internal control over compliance of federal awards sufficient to plan the audit to support a low assessed level of control risk for major programs, including consideration of the risk of material noncompliance (materiality) related to each compliance requirement and major program.
- Inadequate documentation of procedures performed.
- Failure to document required communications with those charged with governance, including proper communication of internal control findings.

Sampling

In the 2019 *Compliance Supplement*, there was a special advisory included on sampling. Appendix VII, *Other Audit Advisories*, reminds auditors that when performing an audit under GAAS, including single audits, that AU-C section 530, *Audit Sampling*, provides auditor requirements and guidance related to an auditor's use of sampling. Failure to follow the standards, including the requirement to determine sample sizes that are sufficient to reduce sampling risk to an acceptably low level, may result in the audit being considered nonconforming by the federal cognizant agency for audit as part of a quality control review. Many firms are using "firm specific guidance" or "rules of thumbs" that are not in compliance with AU-C 530. The advisory reminds people to use the AICPA Audit Guide — *Government Auditing Standards* and Single Audits as well as the AICPA Audit Guide — Audit Sampling, when designing samples to remain compliant.

Audit of compliance

In an audit under the Uniform Guidance, in addition to the requirements of *Government Auditing Standards*, the auditor must determine whether the auditee has complied with federal statutes, regulations, and the terms and conditions of federal awards that may have a direct and material effect on each of its major programs.

The Uniform Guidance compliance audit results in the auditor expressing an opinion on the auditee's compliance with those compliance requirements for each of its major programs. To express such an opinion, the auditor accumulates sufficient, appropriate audit evidence by planning, performing risk assessment procedures, and performing tests of transactions and such other audit procedures as are necessary in support of the auditee's compliance with direct and material compliance requirements, thereby limiting audit risk of noncompliance to an appropriately low level.

The following are common deficiencies related to the auditing of compliance found over the past several years by the AICPA Professional Ethics Division and Peer Review Division as part of investigations of single audit engagements:

- The auditor did not obtain sufficient competent evidential matter to support the opinion on major federal programs. The most frequently seen problems concern the following:
  - Inadequate or missing testing of compliance requirements
  - Use of out-of-date work programs or disclosure checklists that result in audit deficiencies
  - Improper use of dual-purpose testing
  - Inadequately designed procedures
  - Lack of an understanding of the difference between internal control and compliance testing
  - Inappropriate or unsupported sample sizes (or both)
- Failure to calculate materiality for each major program.
- The documentation of procedures performed was inadequate.
- The auditor failed to use or customize an audit program.
- Failure to ensure that the written representations from the audited entity contained all applicable elements including the following: representations tailored to the entity and governmental audit regarding federal awards, and representations covering both years when comparative financial statements are presented. Also, improper consideration of the date of the representations in relation to the audit report.
- Failure to identify and test sufficient and appropriate major programs. These errors were the result of using preliminary expenditures when the final expenditures resulted in an other than low risk type A program, failure to cluster, failure to properly perform type A and type B program risk assessments, failure to group programs with the same CFDA number, and incorrect determination of the auditee as low risk resulting in insufficient coverage.
- Failure to properly conclude and document either that an applicable compliance requirement does not apply to the particular auditee or that noncompliance with the requirements could not have a direct and material effect on a major program.
- Lack of documentation of the consideration of subseqent events related to applicable compliance requirements.
- Failure to select the correct version of part 3 of the OMB *Compliance Supplement* to determine applicable compliance requirements for each major program tested.

Appendix 3A

Major Program Determination Case Study

Case study

Nonprofit Entity's programs and expenditures are listed in the *2020 Summary of Programs by CFDA Number*, which consists of summarized data collected by the auditor.

CFDA	Program title	Funds expenditure	Last year audited	Inherent risk assessment
2020 Summary of programs by CFDA number				
Department of Agriculture				
10.557	Special Supplemental Nutrition Program for Women, Infants, and Children	$ 1,200,000	2019	High
10.559	Summer Food Service Program for Children	$ 300,000	2018	Low
10.572	WIC Farmers' Market Nutrition Program	$ 125,000	2016	Low
10.766	Community Facilities Loans and Grants Cluster	$10,000,000	2019	Low
Department of Justice				
16.527	Supervised Visitation, Safe Havens for Children	$ 400,000	2019 SD	High
16.606	State Criminal Alien Assistance Program	$ 771,000	2018	Low
Environmental Protection Agency				
66.001	Air Pollution Control Program Support	$ 200,000	2019	Low
66.034	Surveys, Studies, Research, Investigations, Demonstrations, and Special Purpose Activities Relating to the Clean Air Act	$ 50,000	2019	High
66.039	National Clean Diesel Emissions Reduction Program	$ 800,000	2019 SD	Moderate
Department of Health and Human Services				
93.052	National Family Caregiver Support, Title III, Part E	$ 1,500,000	2017	Low
93.069	Public Health Emergency Preparedness	$ 600,000	2019 MW	Moderate
93.217	Family Planning Services	$ 250,000	2019 MW	Low
93.243	Substance Abuse and Mental Health Services Projects of Regional and National Significance	$ 150,000	2019	High
93.283	Centers for Disease Control and Prevention Investigations and Technical Assistance	$ 100,000	2019	Low
93.556	Promoting Safe and Stable Families	$ 500,000	2016	High
93.563	Child Support Enforcement	$ 25,000	2019 SD	Moderate

2020 Summary of programs by CFDA number (continued)

CFDA	Program title	Funds expenditure	Last year audited	Inherent risk assessment
93.566	Refugee and Entrant Assistance State Administered Programs	$ 500,000	2019	Low
93.568	Low-Income Home Energy Assistance	$ 250,000	2018	Low
93.667	Social Services Block Grant	$ 1,750,000	2019	Low
93.767	Children's Health Insurance Program	$ 650,000	2019 MW	High
93.914	HIV Emergency Relief Project Grants	$ 2,250,000	2018	Low
93.919	Cooperative Agreements for State-Based Comprehensive Breast and Cervical Cancer Early Detection Programs	$ 2,000,000	2017	Moderate
93.943	Epidemiologic Research Studies of Acquired Immunodeficiency Syndrome (AIDS) and Human Immunodeficiency Virus (HIV) Infection in Selected Population Groups	$ 450,000	2018	Low
93.959	Block Grants for Prevention and Treatment of Substance Abuse	$ 50,000	2015	Low
93.991	Preventive Health and Health Services Block Grant	$ 10,000	2017	High
93.994	Maternal and Child Health Services Block Grant to the States	$ 500,000	2018 SD	Moderate
		$ 25,381,000		

Notes:

All had unmodified opinions on programs.

10.766 is determined to be a loan program.

Material weaknesses were found in programs 93.069, 93.217, and 93.767.

Significant deficiencies were found in programs 16.527, 66.039, 93.563, and 93.994.

Immaterial instances of questioned costs were found in programs 10.572, 93.914, and 93.919.

No findings were found in the remainder of the programs.

No agency had indicated a program high risk.

No agency oversight occurred.

The inherent risk assessment is the assessment you would determine today IF you did an assessment. Not all items may require an assessment.

Government entity does not meet the criteria as a low-risk auditee. In preparing for the audit, answer the following questions:

1. What is the type A threshold? Consider the impact of loan programs.

2. Identify the type A programs.

    Type A programs

3. Identify the low-risk and other than low-risk type A programs.

    Low risk

    Other than low risk

4. What is the maximum number of high-risk, type B programs required to be identified?

5. Which type B programs do not require a risk assessment because they meet the criteria for a relatively small program (that is, are immaterial)?

6. Assuming the risk assessment is performed beginning at the top of the Catalog of Federal Domestic Assistance listing of programs, which type B programs would you considered high risk (and why)?

7. How many type B programs did you risk assess?

8. Which programs would you audit as major programs?

CFDA #	Dollars expended	Type A or B?	Why selected?
	Total must be equal to or greater than $10,152,400 (40% of total expenditures)		

Exempt Organizations Glossary

Governmental terminology

accounting system. The methods and records established to identify, assemble, analyze, classify, record, and report a government's transactions and to maintain accountability for the related assets and liabilities.

accrual basis of accounting. The recording of financial effects on a government of transactions and other events and circumstances that have consequences for the government in the periods in which those transactions, events, and circumstances occur, rather than only in the periods in which cash is received or paid by the government.

ad valorem tax. A tax based on value (such as a property tax).

advance from other funds. An asset account used to record noncurrent portions of a long-term debt owed by one fund to another fund within the same reporting entity. (See **due to other funds** and **interfund receivable/payable**).

appropriation. A legal authorization granted by a legislative body to make expenditures and to incur obligations for specific purposes. An appropriation is usually limited in the amount and time it may be expended.

assigned fund balance. A portion of fund balance that includes amounts that are constrained by the government's intent to be used for specific purposes, but that are neither restricted nor committed.

basis of accounting. A term used to refer to *when* revenues, expenditures, expenses, and transfers, and related assets and liabilities are recognized in the accounts and reported in the financial statements. Specifically, it relates to the timing of the measurements made, regardless of the nature of the measurement. (See **accrual basis of accounting**, **cash basis of accounting**, and **modified accrual basis of accounting**).

bond. A written promise to pay a specified sum of money (the face value or principal amount) at a specified date or dates in the future (the maturity dates[s]), together with periodic interest at a specified rate. Sometimes, however, all or a substantial part of the interest is included in the face value of the security. The difference between a note and bond is that the latter is issued for a longer period and requires greater legal formality.

business type activities. Those activities of a government carried out primarily to provide specific services in exchange for a specific user charge.

capital grants. Grants restricted by the grantor for the acquisition or construction, or both, of capital assets.

capital projects fund. A fund used to account for and report financial resources that are restricted, committed, or assigned to expenditures for capital outlays, including the acquisition or construction of capital facilities and other capital assets. Capital project funds exclude those types of capital-related outflows financed by proprietary funds or for assets that will be held in trust for individuals, private organizations, or other governments.

cash basis of accounting. A basis of accounting that requires the recognition of transactions only when cash is received or disbursed.

committed fund balance. A portion of fund balance that includes amounts that can only be used for specific purposes pursuant to constraints imposed by formal action of the government's highest level of decision-making authority.

consumption method. The method of accounting that requires the recognition of an expenditure or expense as inventories are used.

contributed capital. Contributed capital is created when a general capital asset is transferred to a proprietary fund or when a grant is received that is externally restricted to capital acquisition or construction. Contributions restricted to capital acquisition and construction and capital assets received from developers are reported in the operating statement as a separate item after nonoperating revenues and expenses.

custodial fund. A fiduciary fund used to account for financial resources not administered through a trust or equivalent arrangement meeting specified criteria, and that are not required to be reported in a pension (and other employee benefit) trust fund, investment trust fund, or private-purpose trust fund.

debt service fund. A fund used to account for and report financial resources that are restricted, committed, or assigned to expenditure for principal and interest. Debt service funds should be used to report resources if legally mandated. Financial resources that are being accumulated for principal and interest maturing in future years should also be reported as debt service funds.

deferred inflow of resources. An acquisition of net assets by a government that is applicable to a future reporting period.

deferred outflow of resources. A consumption of net asset by a government that is applicable to a future reporting period.

deficit. (*a*) The excess of the liabilities of a fund over its assets. (*b*) The excess of expenditures over revenues during an accounting period or, in the case of proprietary funds, the excess of expenses over revenues during an accounting period.

disbursement. A payment made in cash or by check. Expenses are only recognized at the time physical cash is disbursed.

due from other funds. A current asset account used to indicate an account reflecting amounts owed to a particular fund by another fund for goods sold or services rendered. This account includes only short-term obligations on an open account, not interfund loans.

due to other funds. A current liability account reflecting amounts owed by a particular fund to another fund for goods sold or services rendered. This account includes only short-term obligations on an open account, not interfund loans.

enabling legislation. Legislation that authorizes a government to assess, levy, charge, or otherwise mandate payment of resources from external resource providers and includes a legally enforceable requirement that those resources be used for the specific purposes stipulated in the legislation.

encumbrances. Commitments related to unperformed (executory) contracts for goods or services. Used in budgeting, encumbrances are not generally accepted accounting principles (GAAP) expenditures or liabilities but represent the estimated amount of expenditures that will ultimately result if unperformed contracts in process are completed.

enterprise fund. A fund established to account for operations financed and operated in a manner similar to private business enterprises (such as gas, utilities, transit systems, and parking garages). Usually, the governing body intends that costs of providing goods or services to the general public be recovered primarily through user charges.

expenditures. Decreases in net financial resources. Expenditures include current operating expenses requiring the present or future use of net current assets, debt service and capital outlays, intergovernmental grants, entitlements, and shared revenues.

expenses. Outflows or other consumption of assets or incurrences of liabilities, or a combination of both, from delivering or producing goods, rendering services, or carrying out other activities that constitute the entity's ongoing major or central operations.

fiduciary fund. A fund that reports fiduciary activities meeting the criteria in paragraphs 6–11 of GASB Statement No. 84, *Fiduciary Activities*. Financial reporting is focused on reporting net position and changes in net position.

fund. A fiscal and accounting entity with a self-balancing set of accounts in which cash and other financial resources, all related liabilities and residual equities, or balances, and changes therein, are recorded and segregated to carry on specific activities or attain certain objectives in accordance with special regulations, restrictions, or limitations.

fund balance. The difference between fund assets and fund liabilities of the generic fund types within the governmental category of funds.

fund financial statements. Each fund has its own set of self-balancing accounts and fund financial statements that focus on information about the government's governmental, proprietary, and fiduciary fund types.

fund type. The 11 generic funds that all transactions of a government are recorded into. The 11 fund types are as follows: general, special revenue, debt service, capital projects, permanent, enterprise, internal service, private-purpose trust, pension (and other employee benefit) trust, investment trust, and custodial.

GASB. The Governmental Accounting Standards Board (GASB), organized in 1984 by the Financial Accounting Foundation (FAF) to establish standards of financial accounting and reporting for state and local governmental entities. Its standards guide the preparation of external financial reports of those entities.

general fund. The fund within the governmental category used to account for all financial resources, except those required to be accounted for in another governmental fund.

general-purpose governments. Governmental entities that provide a range of services, such as states, cities, counties, towns, and villages.

governmental funds. Funds used to account for the acquisition, use, and balances of spendable financial resources and the related current liabilities, except those accounted for in proprietary funds and fiduciary funds. Essentially, these funds are accounting segregations of financial resources. Spendable assets are assigned to a particular government fund type according to the purposes for which they may or must be used. Current liabilities are assigned to the fund type from which they are to be paid. The difference between the assets and liabilities of governmental fund types is referred to as *fund balance*. The measurement focus in these fund types is on the determination of financial position and changes in financial position (sources, uses, and balances of financial resources), rather than on net income determination.

government-wide financial statements. Highly aggregated financial statements that present financial information for all assets (including infrastructure capital assets), liabilities, and net assets of a primary government and its component units, except for fiduciary funds. The government-wide financial statements use the economic resources measurement focus and accrual basis of accounting.

infrastructure assets. Long-lived capital assets that normally are stationary in nature and can be preserved for a significantly greater number of years than most capital assets. Examples of infrastructure assets are roads, bridges, tunnels, drainage systems, water and sewer systems, dams, and lighting systems. Buildings, except those that are an ancillary part of a network of infrastructure assets, are not considered infrastructure assets.

interfund receivable/payable. Activity between funds of a government reflecting amounts provided with a requirement for repayment, or sales and purchases of goods and services between funds approximating their external exchange value (also referred to as **interfund loans** or **interfund services provided and used**).

internal service fund. A generic fund type within the proprietary category used to account for the financing of goods or services provided by one department or agency to other departments or agencies of a government, or to other governments, on a cost-reimbursement basis.

investment trust fund. A generic fund type within the fiduciary category used by a government in a fiduciary capacity, such as to maintain its cash and investment pool for other governments.

major funds. A government's general fund (or its equivalent), other individual governmental type, and enterprise funds that meet specific quantitative criteria, and any other governmental or

---

enterprise fund that a government's officials believe is particularly important to financial statement users.

management's discussion and analysis. Management's discussion and analysis, or MD&A, is required supplementary information that introduces the basic financial statements by presenting certain financial information as well as management's analytical insights on that information.

measurement focus. The accounting convention that determines (*a*) which assets and which liabilities are included on a government's balance sheet and where they are reported, and (*b*) whether an operating statement presents information on the flow of financial resources (revenues and expenditures) or information on the flow of economic resources (revenues and expenses).

modified accrual basis of accounting. The basis of accounting adapted to the governmental fund type measurement focus. Revenues and other financial resource increments are recognized when they become both *measurable* and *available to finance expenditures of the current period*. *Available* means collectible in the current period or soon enough thereafter to be used to pay liabilities of the current period. Expenditures are recognized when the fund liability is incurred and expected to be paid from current resources, except for (*a*) inventories of materials and supplies that may be considered expenditures either when purchased or when used, and (*b*) prepaid insurance and similar items that may be considered expenditures either when paid for or when consumed. All governmental funds are accounted for using the modified accrual basis of accounting in fund financial statements.

modified approach. Rules that allow infrastructure assets that are part of a network or subsystem of a network not to be depreciated as long as certain requirements are met.

net position. The residual of all other elements presented in a statement of financial position.

nonspendable fund balance. The portion of fund balance that includes amounts that cannot be spent because they are either (*a*) not in spendable form or (*b*) legally or contractually required to be maintained intact.

pension (and other employee benefit) trust fund. A trust fund used to account for a public employees retirement system, OPEB plan, or other employee benefits other than pensions that are administered through trusts that meet specified criteria. Pension (and other employee benefit) trust funds use the accrual basis of accounting and the flow of economic resources measurement focus.

permanent fund. A generic fund type under the governmental category used to report resources that are legally restricted to the extent that only earnings, and not principal, may be used for purposes that support the reporting government's programs and, therefore, are for the benefit of the government or its citizenry. (Permanent funds do not include private-purpose trust funds, which should be used when the government is required to use the principal or earnings for the benefit of individuals, private organizations, or other governments).

private purpose trust fund. A general fund type under the fiduciary category used to report resources held and administered by the reporting government acting in a fiduciary capacity for individuals, other governments, or private organizations.

proprietary funds. The government category used to account for a government's ongoing organizations and activities that are similar to those often found in the private sector (these are enterprise and internal service funds). All assets, liabilities, equities, revenues, expenses, and transfers relating to the government's business and quasi-business activities are accounted for through proprietary funds. Proprietary funds should apply all applicable GASB pronouncements and those GAAP applicable to similar businesses in the private sector, unless those conflict with GASB pronouncements. These funds use the accrual basis of accounting in conjunction with the flow of economic resources measurement focus.

purchases method. The method under which inventories are recorded as expenditures when acquired.

restricted fund balance. Portion of fund balance that reflects constraints placed on the use of resources (other than nonspendable items) that are either (a) externally imposed by a creditor, such as through debt covenants, grantors, contributors, or laws or regulations of other governments or (b) imposed by law through constitutional provisions or enabling legislation.

required supplementary information. GAAP specify that certain information be presented as required supplementary information, or RSI.

special-purpose governments. Legally separate entities that perform only one activity or a few activities, such as cemetery districts, school districts, colleges and universities, utilities, hospitals and other health care organizations, and public employee retirement systems.

special revenue fund. A fund that must have revenue or proceeds from specific revenue sources that are either restricted or committed for a specific purpose other than debt service or capital projects. This definition means that in order to be considered a special revenue fund, there must be one or more revenue sources upon which reporting the activity in a separate fund is predicated.

interfund transfers. All transfers, such as legally authorized transfers from a fund receiving revenue to a fund through which the resources are to be expended, where there is no intent to repay. Interfund transfers are recorded on the operating statement.

unassigned fund balance. Residual classification for the general fund. This classification represents fund balance that has not been assigned to other funds and has not been restricted, committed, or assigned to specific purposes within the general fund. The general fund should be the only fund that reports a positive unassigned fund balance amount. In other funds, if expenditures incurred for specific purposes exceeded the amounts restricted, committed, or assigned to those purposes, it may be necessary to report a negative unassigned fund balance.

unrestricted fund balance. The total of committed fund balance, assigned fund balance, and unassigned fund balance.

Not-for-profit terminology

board-designated endowment fund. An endowment fund created by a not-for-profit entity's governing board by designating a portion of its net assets without donor restrictions to be invested to provide income for a long, but not necessarily specified, period. In rare circumstances, a board-designated endowment fund also can include a portion of net assets with donor restrictions. For example, if a not-for-profit is unable to spend donor-restricted contributions in the near term, then the board sometimes considers the long-term investment of these funds.

board-designated net assets. Net assets without donor restrictions subject to self-imposed limits by action of the governing board. Board-designated net assets may be earmarked for future programs, investment, contingencies, purchase or construction of fixed assets, or other uses. Some governing boards may delegate designation decisions to internal management. Such designations are considered to be included in board-designated net assets.

charitable lead trust. A trust established in connection with a split-interest agreement in which the not-for-profit entity receives distributions during the agreement's term. Upon termination of the trust, the remainder of the trust assets are paid to the donor or to third-party beneficiaries designated by the donor.

charitable remainder trust. A trust established in connection with a split-interest agreement in which the donor or a third-party beneficiary receives specified distributions during the agreement's term. Upon termination of the trust, a not-for-profit entity receives the assets remaining in the trust.

collections. Works of art, historical treasures, or similar assets that are (*a*) held for public exhibition, education, or research in furtherance of public service, rather than financial gain; (*b*) protected, kept unencumbered, cared for, and preserved; and (*c*) subject to an organizational policy that requires the proceeds of items that are sold to be used to acquire other items for collections.

conditional promise to give. A promise to give that is subject to a donor-imposed condition.

contribution. An unconditional transfer of cash or other assets, as well as unconditional promises to give, to an entity or a reduction, settlement, or cancellation of its liabilities in a voluntary nonreciprocal transfer by another entity acting other than as an owner.

costs of joint activities. Costs incurred for a joint activity. Costs of joint activities may include joint costs and costs other than joint costs. *Costs other than joint costs* are costs that are identifiable with a particular function, such as program, fund-raising, management and general, and membership development costs.

donor-imposed restriction. A donor stipulation (*donors* include other types of contributors, including makers of certain grants) that specifies a use for the contributed asset that is more specific than broad limits resulting from the nature of the organization, the environment in which it operates, and the purposes specified in its articles of incorporation or bylaws, or comparable documents for an unincorporated association. A restriction on an organization's use of the asset contributed may be temporary in nature or perpetual in nature.

donor-restricted endowment fund. An endowment fund that is created by a donor stipulation (*donors* include other types of contributors, including makers of certain grants) that requires investment of the gift in perpetuity or for a specified term. Some donors or laws may require that a portion of income, gains, or both be added to the gift and invested subject to similar restrictions.

donor-restricted support. Donor-restricted revenues or gains from contributions that increase net assets with donor restrictions (*donors* include other types of contributions, including makers of certain grants).

economic interest. A not-for-profit entity's interest in another entity that exists if any of the following criteria are met: (*a*) The other entity holds or uses significant resources that must be used for the purposes of the not-for-profit entity, either directly or indirectly, by producing income or providing services, or (*b*) the not-for-profit entity is responsible for the liabilities of the other entity.

endowment fund. An established fund of cash, securities, or other assets that provides income for the maintenance of a not-for-profit entity. The use of the assets of the fund may be with or without donor-imposed restrictions. Endowment funds generally are established by donor-restricted gifts and bequests to provide a source of income.

functional expense classification. A method of grouping expenses according to the purpose for which the costs are incurred. The primary functional classifications of a not-for-profit entity are program services and supporting activities.

funds functioning as endowment. Net assets without donor restrictions (*donors* include other types of contributors, including makers of certain grants) designated by an entity's governing board to be invested to provide income for generally a long, but not necessarily specified, period.

joint activity. An activity that is part of the fund-raising function and has elements of one or more other functions, such as programs, management and general, membership development, or any other functional category used by the entity.

joint costs. The costs of conducting joint activities that are not identifiable with a particular component of the activity.

management and general activities. Supporting activities that are not directly identifiable with one or more programs, fund-raising activities, or membership development activities.

natural expense classification. A method of grouping expenses according to the kinds of economic benefits received in incurring those expenses. Examples of natural expense classifications include salaries and wages, employee benefits, professional services, supplies, interest expense, rent, utilities, and depreciation.

net assets. The excess or deficiency of assets over liabilities of a not-for-profit entity, which is divided into two mutually exclusive classes according to the existence or absence of donor-imposed restrictions.

net assets with donor restrictions. The part of net assets of a not-for-profit entity that is subject to donor-imposed restrictions (*donors* include other types of contributors, including makers of certain grants).

net assets without donor restrictions. The part of net assets of a not-for-profit entity that is not subject to donor-imposed restrictions (*donors* include other types of contributors, including makers of certain grants).

programmatic investing. The activity of making loans or other investments that are directed at carrying out a not-for-profit entity's purpose for existence, rather than investing in the general production of income or appreciation of an asset (for example, total return investing). An example of programmatic investing is a loan made to lower-income individuals to promote home ownership.

promise to give. A written or oral agreement to contribute cash or other assets to another entity. A promise to give may be either conditional or unconditional.

underwater endowment fund. A donor-restricted endowment fund for which the fair value of the fund at the reporting date is less than either the original gift amount or the amount required to be maintained by the donor or by law that extends donor restrictions.

Single audit and Yellow Book terminology

attestation engagements. Attestation engagements concern examining, reviewing, or performing agreed-upon procedures on a subject matter or an assertion about a subject matter and reporting on the results.

compliance supplement. A document issued annually in the spring by the OMB to provide guidance to auditors.

data collection form. A form submitted to the Federal Audit Clearinghouse that provides information about the auditor, the auditee and its federal programs, and the results of the audit.

federal financial assistance. Assistance that nonfederal entities receive or administer in the form of grants, loans, loan guarantees, property, cooperative agreements, interest subsidies, insurance, food commodities, direct appropriations, or other assistance, but does not include amounts received as reimbursement for services rendered to individuals in accordance with guidance issued by the director.

financial audits. Financial audits are primarily concerned with providing reasonable assurance about whether financial statements are presented fairly, in all material respects, in conformity with GAAP or with a comprehensive basis of accounting other than GAAP.

GAGAS. Generally accepted government auditing standards issued by the GAO. They are published as *Government Auditing Standards*, also commonly known as the Yellow Book.

GAO. The United States Government Accountability Office. Among its responsibilities is the issuance of GAGAS.

OMB. The Office of Management and Budget. The OMB assists the President in the development and implementation of budget, program, management, and regulatory policies.

pass-through entity. A nonfederal entity that provides federal awards to a subrecipient to carry out a federal program.

performance audits. Performance audits entail an objective and systematic examination of evidence to provide an independent assessment of the performance and management of a program against objective criteria as well as assessments that provide a prospective focus or that synthesize information on best practices or cross-cutting issues.

program-specific audit. A compliance audit of one federal program.

single audit. An audit of a nonfederal entity that includes the entity's financial statements and federal awards.

single audit guide. This AICPA Audit Guide, formally titled Government Auditing Standards *and Single Audits*, is the former Statement of Position (SOP) 98-3, *Audits of States, Local Governments, and Not-for-Profit Organizations Receiving Federal Awards*. The single audit guide provides guidance on the auditor's responsibilities when conducting a single audit or program-specific audit in accordance with the Single Audit Act, GAGAS, and the Uniform Guidance.

subrecipient. A nonfederal entity that receives federal awards through another nonfederal entity to carry out a federal program but does not include an individual who receives financial assistance through such awards.

Uniform Guidance. Formally known as Title 2 U.S. *Code of Federal Regulations* Part 200, *Uniform Administrative Requirements, Cost Principles, and Audit Requirements for Federal Awards*. The Uniform Guidance sets forth the requirements for the compliance audit portion of a single audit.

Index

2020 NOT-FOR-PROFIT ACCOUNTING AND AUDITING UPDATE

By Melisa F. Galasso, CPA

Solutions

The AICPA publishes *CPA Letter Daily*, a free e-newsletter published each weekday. The newsletter, which covers the 10-12 most important stories in business, finance, and accounting, as well as AICPA information, was created to deliver news to CPAs and others who work with the accounting profession. Besides summarizing media articles, commentaries, and research results, the e-newsletter links to television broadcasts and videos and features reader polls. *CPA Letter Daily*'s editors scan hundreds of publications and websites, selecting the most relevant and important news so you don't have to. The newsletter arrives in your inbox early in the morning. To sign up, visit_smartbrief.com/CPA.

Do you need high-quality technical assistance? The AICPA Auditing and Accounting Technical Hotline provides non-authoritative guidance on accounting, auditing, attestation, and compilation and review standards. The hotline can be reached at 877.242.7212.

Solutions

Chapter 1

Knowledge check solutions

1.
   a. Correct. The "Opinion" section now goes first.
   b. Incorrect. The "Basis for Opinion" follows the "Opinion" section.
   c. Incorrect. The "Responsibilities of Management" section follows the "Opinion" and "Basis of Opinion" paragraphs.
   d. Incorrect. "Auditor's Responsibilities for the Audit of the Financial Statements" follows the "Responsibilities of Management" section.

2.
   a. Incorrect. When issuing a qualified opinion, you do have to include basis for opinion paragraphs.
   b. Incorrect. The basis for opinion section has one paragraph in an unmodified opinion.
   c. Correct. There are two paragraphs in the basis for opinion section when issuing a qualified opinion.
   d. Incorrect. There are not three paragraphs in the basis for opinion section.

3.
   a. Correct. AU-C section 701 introduces key audit matters (KAM).
   b. Incorrect. The PCAOB uses the term critical audit matters.
   c. Incorrect. Significant audit matters are not introduced in AU-C section 701.
   d. Incorrect. Crucial audit matters are not introduced in AU-C section 701.

4.
   a. Correct. SAS No. 135 does converge with AS 1301.
   b. Incorrect. SAS No. 135 does not converge with AS 2701.
   c. Incorrect. SAS No. 135 does not converge with AS 1005.
   d. Incorrect. AS 2570 is not a PCAOB standard.

5.

    a. Incorrect. The word "is" is not a key change in the definition of materiality.

    b. Correct. The word "could" is a key change in the definition of materiality.

    c. Incorrect. The word "will" is not a key change in the definition of materiality.

    d. Incorrect. The word "for" is not a key change in the definition of materiality.

6.

    a. Incorrect. Examinations are not addressed in SSAE 19.

    b. Incorrect. Review engagements are not addressed in SSAE 19.

    c. Correct. AUPs are updated in SSAE 19.

    d. Incorrect. Compilations are not subject to the SSAEs.

7.

    a. Incorrect. Using an API to translate is not a prohibited non-attest service.

    b. Incorrect. Providing distinct network support is not a prohibited non-attest service.

    c. Correct. Developing a FIS is a prohibited non-attest service.

    d. Incorrect. Installing a FIS is not a prohibited non-attest service.

8.

    a. Incorrect. More than 25% were nonconforming.

    b. Incorrect. More than 35% were nonconforming.

    c. Incorrect. More than 45% were nonconforming.

    d. Correct. Fifty-five percent were nonconforming.

9.

    a. Incorrect. Final assembly is not required to be performed within 45 days following the audit report date.

    b. Incorrect. Final assembly is not required to be performed within 60 days following the audit report date.

    c. Incorrect. Final assembly is not required to be performed within 45 days following the report release date.

    d. Correct. Final assembly is required to be performed within 60 days following the report release date.

Appendix A Case study

Part 1

Example 1:

Did the auditor document:	YES	NO
1. The nature and extent of the procedures?		✓
2. The timing of the procedures?	✓	
3. The results of the procedures?		✓

- Has the auditor documented the nature and extent of the procedures, including the identifying characteristics of the items tested?
  - No. Although we know which assertions the auditor tested, we really have no idea what the auditor did to test them.
- Has the auditor documented the timing of the procedures?
  - Yes, both the preparer and reviewer have signed off and dated, so we know who did the work, who reviewed it, and when it happened.
- Has the auditor documented the results of the procedures?
  - No. We don't know what the auditor did to test the assertions, let alone what the results were.
- Key point:
  - Checklists can be used to facilitate audit procedures but checking off a step in an audit program or a checklist will rarely provide sufficient documentation about the nature, timing and extent of audit procedures performed, the evidence obtained or the results of the procedures.

Example 2

Did the auditor document:	YES	NO
1. The nature and extent of the procedures?	✓	
2. The timing of the procedures?	✓	
3. The results of the procedures?	✓	

- Has the auditor documented the nature and extent of the procedures, including the identifying characteristics of the items tested?
    - Yes. We know the auditor obtained the firm's only note and reviewed it.
    - We also know that the auditor obtained a confirmation letter from the borrower.
    - Finally, we know that the auditor traced the balance of the note back to the trial balance.
- Has the auditor documented the timing of the procedures?
    - Yes, both the preparer and reviewer have signed off and dated, so we know who did the work, who reviewed it, and when it happened.
- Has the auditor documented the results of the procedures?
    - Yes.
        - The auditor verified that the note exists, and the client is the note holder.
        - The borrower confirmed the balance and maturity date of the note.
        - The balance of the note traced back to the trial balance.
- Key point:
    - Documentation does not have to be painful. A short note on an audit program can be sufficient to meet the requirements of the standard.

Part 2

Example 3

Did the auditor document:	YES	NO
1. The nature and extent of the procedures?		✓
2. The timing of the procedures?	✓	
3. The results of the procedures?		✓

- Has the auditor documented the nature and extent of the procedures, including the identifying characteristics of the items tested?
    - No. Although we know which items were tested (all notes over $70k) and which assertions were tested, we really have no idea what the auditor did to test them.
- Has the auditor documented the timing of the procedures?
    - Yes, both the preparer and reviewer have signed off and dated, so we know who did the work, who reviewed it, and when it happened.
- Has the auditor documented the results of the procedures?
    - No. We don't know what the auditor did to test the assertions, let alone what the results were.
- Key point:
    - Although a short note may be appropriate to document certain low-complexity procedures, detail testing of multiple items often requires the development of a schedule.

Example 4

Did the auditor document:	YES	NO
1. The nature and extent of the procedures?	✓	
2. The timing of the procedures?	✓	
3. The results of the procedures?	✓	

- This time, the auditor developed a schedule to provide evidence of the procedures they performed and their results.
- The auditor documented the nature, extent, timing and results of the procedure by
  - clearly laying out the objective,
  - identifying the specific items to be tested (notes from Customers A, B, C and D),
  - using tick marks to indicate that note amounts were traced to confirmations, and a schedule of notes which ties to the trial balance, and
  - signing off and dating the working paper.

Appendix B Case study solution

Part 1 — Exercise: Draw a line to the corresponding section header for each statement below. Solutions are in Red.

Basis for opinion — We believe that the audit evidence we have obtained is sufficient and appropriate to provide a basis for our audit opinion.

Auditor's responsibilities — Misstatements are considered material if there is a substantial likelihood that, individually or in the aggregate, they would influence the judgment made by a reasonable user based on the financial statements.

Key Audit Matters — Key audit matters are those matters that were communicated with those charged with governance and, in our professional judgment, were of most significance in our audit of the financial statements of the current period.

Opinion — In our opinion, the accompanying financial statements present fairly, in all material respects, the financial position of NFP Entity as of December 31, 20X1 and 20X0, and the results of its operations and its cash flows for the years then ended in accordance with accounting principles generally accepted in the United States of America.

Auditor's responsibilities — Reasonable assurance is a high level of assurance but is not absolute assurance and therefore is not a guarantee that an audit conducted in accordance with GAAS will always detect a material misstatement when it exists.

Basis for opinion — We are required to be independent of ABC Company and to meet our other ethical responsibilities, in accordance with the relevant ethical requirements relating to our audits.

Opinion — We have audited the financial statements of NFP Entity, which comprise the balance sheets as of December 31, 20X1 and 20X0, and the related statements of income, changes in stockholders' equity, and cash flows for the years then ended, and the related notes to the financial statements.

Key audit matters — These matters were addressed in the context of our audit of the financial statements as a whole, and in forming our opinion thereon, and we do not provide a separate opinion on these matters. Our objectives are to obtain reasonable assurance about whether the financial statements as a whole are free from material misstatement, whether due to fraud or error, and to issue an auditor's report that includes our opinion.

Auditor's responsibilities — The risk of not detecting a material misstatement resulting from fraud is higher than for one resulting from error, as fraud may involve collusion, forgery, intentional omissions, misrepresentations, or the override of internal control.

Basis for opinion — We conducted our audits in accordance with auditing standards generally accepted in the United States of America (GAAS).

Part 2 — Based on the updated report in SAS 134, fill in the blank with the word(s) that properly completes the sentence:

Exercise professional __judgment_____ and maintain professional skepticism throughout the audit.

Identify and __assess____ the risks of material misstatement of the financial statements, whether due to fraud or ___error___, and design and perform audit procedures responsive to those risks.

Obtain an __understanding_____ of internal control relevant to the audit in order to design audit procedures that are appropriate in the circumstances, but not for the purpose of expressing an opinion on the effectiveness of the ABC Company's internal control.

Evaluate the __appropriateness_____ of accounting policies used and the reasonableness of significant accounting estimates made by management, as well as evaluate the overall ___presentation_____ of the financial statements.

Conclude whether, in our judgment, there are conditions or events, considered in the ___aggregate_____, that raise substantial doubt about ABC Company's ability to continue as a going concern for a _____reasonable_____ period of time.

In our opinion, the accompanying financial statements present fairly, in all __material_____ respects, the financial position of NFP Entity as of December 31, 20X1 and 20X0, and the results of its operations and its cash flows for the years then ended in accordance with accounting principles generally accepted in the United States of America.

Key audit matters are those matters that were communicated with those charged with governance and, in our professional judgment, were of most ___significance_____ in our audit of the financial statements of the current period.

Management is responsible for the __preparation_____ and fair presentation of the financial statements in accordance with accounting principles generally accepted in the United States of America, and for the design, implementation, and ___maintenance_____ of internal control relevant to the preparation and fair presentation of financial statements that are free from material misstatement, whether due to __fraud_____ or ___error_____.

In preparing the financial statements, ___mangement_____ is required to evaluate whether there are conditions or events, considered in the aggregate, that raise substantial doubt about the Company's ability to continue as a going concern for [insert the time period set by the applicable financial reporting framework].

Our __objectives____ are to obtain __reasonable_____ assurance about whether the financial statements as a whole are free from material misstatement, whether due to fraud or error, and to issue an auditor's report that includes our ___opinion_____.

___Reasonable_____ assurance is a ___high____ level of assurance but is not _absolute_____ assurance and therefore is not a guarantee that an audit conducted in accordance with GAAS will __always___ detect a material misstatement when it exists.

The risk of not detecting a material misstatement resulting from __fraud__ is higher than for one resulting from __error___, as fraud may involve collusion, forgery, intentional omissions, misrepresentations, or the override of internal control.

Chapter 2

Knowledge check solutions

1.
   a. Incorrect. Grants that are determined to be exchange transactions are in scope.
   b. Incorrect. Sales from a NFP's store is in scope.
   c. Correct. Donor contributions are not in scope.
   d. Incorrect. Sponsorships that are part exchange and part contribution are in scope.

2.

  a. Incorrect. Performance obligations are not required to be discrete.
  b. Correct. Performance obligations must be distinct.
  c. Incorrect. Performance obligations are not required to be divergent.
  d. Incorrect. Performance obligations are not required to be disparate.

3.

  a. Incorrect. Exchange transactions are not when participants receive equal value.
  b. Correct. Exchange transactions are when participants receive commensurate value.
  c. Incorrect. Exchange transactions are not when participants receive equivalent value.
  d. Incorrect. Exchange transactions are not when participants receive proportionate value.

4.

  a. Incorrect. Measurable performance-related barrier or other measurable barrier is a barrier.
  b. Incorrect. Limited discretion by the recipient on the conduct of an activity is a barrier.
  c. Incorrect. Stipulations that are related to the purpose of the agreement is a barrier.
  d. Correct. The extent to which a stipulation requires additional action is not a barrier.

5.

  a. Incorrect. Capital leases are not a category of a lease in ASU No. 2016-02.
  b. Correct. Finance leases are a category of leases in ASU No. 2016-02.
  c. Incorrect. Investing leases are not a category of a lease in ASU No. 2016-02.
  d. Incorrect. Quasi leases are not a category of a lease in ASU No. 2016-02.

6.

  a. Incorrect. Operating leases do not result in the recognition of interest expense.
  b. Incorrect. Operating leases do not result in the recognition of amortization expense.
  c. Correct. Operating leases result in the recognition of a single lease cost.
  d. Incorrect. Operating leases do not result in the recognition of depreciation expense.

7.

  a. Incorrect. Held to maturity debt securities are affected by ASU No. 2016-13.
  b. Incorrect. Available for sale debt securities are affected by ASU No. 2016-13.
  c. Incorrect. Accounts receivable are affected by ASU No. 2016-13.
  d. Correct. Trading securities are not affected by ASU No. 2016-13.

8.

- a. Incorrect. Debt extinguishment costs should not be presented in operating activities.
- b. Incorrect. Debt extinguishment costs should not be presented in investing activities.
- c. Correct. Debt extinguishment costs should be presented in financing activities.
- d. Incorrect. Debt extinguishment costs should not be presented as noncash activities.

9.

- a. Correct. Restricted cash transactions should be presented as either operating, investing, or financing cash flows.
- b. Incorrect. Restricted cash transactions should be presented on the cash flow statement.
- c. Incorrect. Restricted cash transactions should not only be disclosed in the notes.
- d. Incorrect. Restricted cash transactions should be presented as a noncash activity.

10.

- a. Incorrect. ASU No. 2017-04 did not remove step 0.
- b. Incorrect. ASU No. 2017-04 did not remove step 1.
- c. Correct. ASU No. 2017-04 removed step 2.
- d. Incorrect. There is no such thing as step 3.

11.

- a. Correct. ASU No. 2017-07 permits the capitalization of service cost.
- b. Incorrect. ASU No. 2017-07 does not permit the capitalization of interest cost.
- c. Incorrect. ASU No. 2017-07 does not permit the capitalization of the expected return on plan assets for the period.
- d. Incorrect. ASU No. 2017-07 does not permit the capitalization of the prior service cost or credit component.

12.

- a. Incorrect. The premium should be amortized more than one year.
- b. Correct. The premium should be amortized over five years.
- c. Incorrect. The premium should be amortized less than nine years.
- d. Incorrect. The premium should be amortized less than 10 years.

Appendix A Case study solution

Part 1

Scenario 1

Because the results of the clinical trial have particular commercial value for the pharmaceutical entity, Pharma Inc. is receiving commensurate value as the resource provider. Therefore, the receipt of the resources is not a contribution received by NFP University, nor is the disbursement of the resources a contribution made by the pharmaceutical entity.

Scenario 2

The grant was awarded to the student, not to the university. The university entered into an exchange transaction with the student and accounts for the $45,000 of revenue in accordance with the guidance in the appropriate subtopic. The $20,000 grant does not create additional revenue but, rather, serves as a partial payment against the $45,000 due to CPA University. Jane Hoya, who is receiving the benefit from the grant transaction, is an identified customer of CPA University. This is an example of the third-party payer scope exception.

Scenario 3

Motion NFP concludes that this is a procurement arrangement in which commensurate value is being exchanged between two parties and, it should follow the relevant guidance for exchange transactions. The key determining factor are the following:

- Motion NFP is paid to perform a research study for the county and turn over a summary of the findings.
- The county retains the rights to the study.

Scenario 4

ReSurch University concludes that this grant is not a transaction in which there is commensurate value being exchanged. The federal government, as the resource provider, does not receive direct commensurate value in exchange for the assets provided because the university retains all rights to the research and findings. ReSurch University and the public receive the primary benefit of any findings. The federal government only receives an indirect benefit because the research and findings serve the general public. Thus, ReSurch University determines that this grant should be accounted for as contribution.

Part 2

Scenario 1

Workvets determines that it should account for this grant as conditional. The agreement contains a right of release from obligation because the resource provider will only transfer assets if Workvets provides training to at least 4,000 disabled veterans during the year (with a minimum requirement of 1,000 per quarter) as specified in the agreement. The foundation requires Workvets to achieve a specific level of service that would be considered a measurable performance-related barrier (in the form of milestones by specifying the number of veterans that must be served per quarter). In this example, Workvets' entitlement to the transferred assets is contingent upon meeting minimum service requirements. The likelihood of serving at least 1,000 disabled veterans for the quarter is not a consideration from the perspective of either the foundation or the NFP when assessing whether the contribution contains a barrier, and is deemed conditional.

Scenario 2

Sealand Grace determines that this grant is conditional. The grant agreement limits the hospital's discretion as a result of the specific requirements on how it may spend the assets (incurring certain qualifying). The grant also includes a release from the promisor's obligation for unused assets. The requirement to spend the assets on qualifying expenses is a barrier to entitlement because the requirement limits Sealand Grace's discretion about how to use the assets, and the assets would need to be spent on specific items on the basis of the requirements of the agreement (for example, adherence to cost principles) before the hospital is entitled to the assets. This is in contrast to a restriction that typically places limits only on a specific activity that is being funded. Sealand Grace records revenue during the grant period when the barriers have been overcome as it incurs qualifying expenses. The likelihood of incurring qualifying expenses is not a consideration when assessing whether the contribution is deemed conditional.

Scenario 3

ECO Watch determines that the grant is not a conditional contribution. The purpose of research on Asian Carp results in donor-restricted revenue because the purpose of the grant (studying the impact of Asian Carp in the Great Lakes) is narrower than the overall mission of the entity. There are no requirements in the agreement that would indicate that a barrier exists, which must be overcome before the recipient is entitled to the resources. ECO Watch also determines that the reporting requirement alone is not a barrier because it is an administrative requirement and not related to the purpose of the agreement, which is the actual research. This is an example in which a grant including a right of return could not be considered conditional because the return clause is not coupled with a barrier to be overcome, as determined by ECO Watch using judgment to assess the indicators of a barrier.

Scenario 4

The adoption center determines that this grant is conditional. The grant includes a measurable barrier (2,000 additional square feet) that must be achieved in order to be entitled to the assets and a right of return for unused assets or unmet requirements.

Scenario 5

Accountown University determines that this grant is not conditional because the agreement places limits only on the specific activity that is being funded (for example, the assets can be used toward the new building or toward other capital improvements, such as roofing or communications upgrades in existing buildings on campus). The resource provider does not include any specifications about how the building should be constructed as the agreement only indicates that the university must use the grant for the purpose outlined in the capital campaign materials. Accountown University recognizes this grant as donor-restricted revenue because it must be used for capital purposes, which is narrower than the university's overall mission. This example illustrates a fact pattern in which a grant can include a right of return and would be deemed a contribution that does not contain a donor-imposed condition because the return clause is not coupled with a barrier to be overcome, as determined by Accountown University using judgment to assess the indicators of a barrier.

Chapter 3

Knowledge check solutions

1.

    a. Incorrect. The Uniform Guidance contains subpart B, "General Provisions."

    b. Incorrect. The Uniform Guidance contains subpart D, "Post Federal Award Requirements."

    c. Correct. The Uniform Guidance does not contain a subpart G, "Hospital Cost Principles." Hospital Cost Principles are found in appendix IX to Part 200.

    d. Incorrect. The Uniform Guidance contains subpart E, "Cost Principles."

2.

    a. Incorrect. A nonfederal entity that expends $750,000 or more in federal awards during the entity's fiscal year is required to have a single audit.

    b. Incorrect. A nonfederal entity that expends $750,000 or more in federal awards during the entity's fiscal year is required to have a single audit ($500,00 was the threshold under Circular A-133).

    c. Correct. A nonfederal entity that expends $750,000 or more in federal awards during the entity's fiscal year must have a single audit.

    d. Incorrect. A nonfederal entity is required to have a single audit if it expends $750,000 or more in federal awards during the entity's fiscal year.

3.

    a. Incorrect. A large loan program is a federal program providing loans that exceeds four times (not two times) the largest nonloan program.

    b. Incorrect. A large loan program is a federal program providing loans that exceeds four times (not three times) the largest nonloan program.

    c. Correct. A large loan program is a federal program providing loans that exceeds four times the largest nonloan program.

    d. Incorrect. A large loan program is a federal program providing loans that exceeds four times (not five times) the largest nonloan program.

4.

   a. Incorrect. Type A programs do not allow for more professional judgment than type B programs.

   b. Correct. Type A programs allow for less professional judgment than type B programs.

   c. Incorrect. Type A programs do not allow for the same amount of professional judgment than type B programs.

   d. Incorrect. Professional judgment is permitted in major program determination.

5.

   a. Incorrect. A small type B program threshold is based on a percentage of the type A threshold — not a dollar amount.

   b. Incorrect. A small type B program threshold is based on a percentage of the type A threshold — not a dollar amount.

   c. Correct. A small type B program is one that is 25% or less of the type A threshold.

   d. Incorrect. A small type B program is one that is 25% or less of the type A threshold.

6.

   a. Incorrect. The corrective action plan is a separate document from the schedule of finding and questioned cost.

   b. Correct. The corrective action plan must be prepared by the auditee.

   c. Incorrect. The corrective action plan is not the responsibility of the auditor; it is the responsibility of the auditee.

   d. Incorrect. The corrective action plan is not optional.

7.

   a. Correct. Procurement by macro-purchases is not an acceptable method.

   b. Incorrect. Procurement by small purchase procedures is an acceptable method.

   c. Incorrect. Procurement by sealed bid is an acceptable method.

   d. Incorrect. Noncompetitive proposal is an acceptable method.

8.

   a. Incorrect. The Uniform Guidance does not include cost principles applicable to hospitals.

   b. Incorrect. Some nonfederal entities may have awards subject to pre-Uniform Guidance requirements.

   c. Incorrect. Uniform Guidance requirements, including cost principles, are not applicable to for-profit entities.

   d. Correct. A direct cost is defined as one that can be specifically identified with a particular cost objective, such as a federal award.

Federal activities case study

Case study

Solution

Government Entity programs and expenditures are listed in the *2020 Summary of Programs by CFDA Number*, which consists of summarized data collected by the auditor. Government Entity does not meet the criteria as a low-risk auditee. In preparing for the audit, answer the following questions:

1. What is the type A threshold? $750,000 (10.766 is a large loan program, as such it is removed from the total expenditures when determining the type A threshold)

2. Identify the type A programs:

Type A programs	10.557, 10.766, 16.606, 66.039, 93.052, 93.667, 93.914, 93.919

3. Identify the low-risk and other than low-risk type A programs:

Low risk	10.557, 10.766, 16.606, 66.039, 93.667, 93.914 (Note—Inherent risk is not a criterion that can be used in determining risk of type A programs.)
Other than low risk	93.052, 93.919

4. What is the maximum number of high-risk type B programs required to be identified?

Required number is: 6 low-risk type A programs × 0.25 = 2 (rounded)

5. Which type B programs do not require a risk assessment because they meet the criteria for a relatively small program (that is, are immaterial)?

10.572, 66.034, 93.243, 93.283, 93.563, 93.959, 93.991

6. Assuming the risk assessment is performed beginning at the top of the CFDA listing of programs, which type B programs would you consider high risk (and why)?

[The answers may vary due to auditor judgment. Also, starting at the top of the list is not the only way to begin the risk assessment process. For example, some auditors may look at highest dollars first, or some other risk factor. In any case, the solution that follows will give an indication of the types of things an auditor may consider in determining high-risk type B programs.]

> High-risk type B program # 1: CFDA # 16.527 with expenditures of $400,000
>
> The program was assessed as high inherent risk and had a significant deficiency in 2019.
>
> High-risk type B program # 2: CFDA # 93.069 with expenditures of $600,000
>
> The program has been assessed as moderately risky and had a material weakness in 2019.
>
> Programs assessed for risk with no conclusion of high risk are 10.559, 66.001. This conclusion was based on an assessment of low inherent risk and no recent findings. Programs not required to be assessed for risk because they have expenditures below the threshold of $187,000 are 10.572, 66.034.

[The auditor is not required to identify more high-risk type B programs than one-quarter the number of low-risk type A programs. That requirement is now met, and risk assessment should stop.]

7. How many type B programs did you risk assess?

   The number of programs assessed for risk in this scenario is four.

8. Which programs would you audit as major programs?

CFDA #	Dollars expended	Type A or B?	Why selected?
93.052	$1,500,000	A	Has not been audited in either of the prior two fiscal periods
93.919	$2,000,000	A	Has not been audited in either of the prior two fiscal periods
16.527	$400,000	B	Determined to be high-risk as part of type B program risk assessment
93.069	$600,000	B	Determined to be high-risk as part of type B program risk assessment

Additional programs of your choice should be selected to test as major programs such that total expenditures being audited as major programs equal or exceed 40 percent of federal awards expended.
($25,381,000 × 0.40 = $10,152,400) They can be selected in any manner the auditor chooses.

The AICPA publishes *CPA Letter Daily*, a free e-newsletter published each weekday. The newsletter, which covers the 10-12 most important stories in business, finance, and accounting, as well as AICPA information, was created to deliver news to CPAs and others who work with the accounting profession. Besides summarizing media articles, commentaries, and research results, the e-newsletter links to television broadcasts and videos and features reader polls. *CPA Letter Daily*'s editors scan hundreds of publications and websites, selecting the most relevant and important news so you don't have to. The newsletter arrives in your inbox early in the morning. To sign up, visit smartbrief.com/CPA.

Do you need high-quality technical assistance? The AICPA Auditing and Accounting Technical Hotline provides non-authoritative guidance on accounting, auditing, attestation, and compilation and review standards. The hotline can be reached at 877.242.7212.

Learn More

Continuing Professional Education

Thank you for selecting the Association of International Certified Professional Accountants as your continuing professional education provider. We have a diverse offering of CPE courses to help you expand your skill set and develop your competencies. Choose from hundreds of different titles spanning the major subject matter areas relevant to CPAs and CGMAs, including

- governmental and not-for-profit accounting, auditing, and updates;
- internal control and fraud;
- audits of employee benefit plans and 401(k) plans;
- individual and corporate tax updates; and
- a vast array of courses in other areas of accounting and auditing, controllership, management, consulting, taxation, and more!

Get your CPE when and where you want

- Self-study learning options that include on-demand, webcasts, and text formats with superior quality and a broad portfolio of topics, including bundled products like –
  - CPExpress® online learning for immediate access to hundreds of one- to four-credit hour online courses for just-in-time learning at a price that is right.
  - Annual Webcast Pass offering live Q&A with experts and unlimited access to the scheduled lineup, all at an incredible discount.
- Staff training programs for audit, tax and preparation, compilation, and review.
- Certificate programs offering comprehensive curriculums developed by practicing experts to build fundamental core competencies in specialized topics.
- National conferences presented by recognized experts.
- Affordable courses on-site at your organization – visit **aicpalearning.org/on-site** for more information.
- Seminars sponsored by your state society and led by top instructors. For a complete list, visit **aicpalearning.org/publicseminar**.

Take control of your career development

The Association's Competency and Learning website at **https://competency.aicpa.org** brings together a variety of learning resources and a self-assessment tool, enabling tracking and reporting of progress toward learning goals.

Visit **www.AICPAStore.com** to browse our CPE selections.

CPExpress® online learning

CPExpress® from the Association of International Certified Professional Accountants combines quality learning with easy online access to deliver convenient, flexible, and affordable learning that fits your busy schedule. Reach your professional development goals with immediate access to hundreds of one- to four-credit hour CPE courses designed to inform, educate, and reinforce the core competencies of the accounting profession. With CPExpress, you

- have unlimited access to hundreds of self-study courses and 500+ CPE hours of training, including regular updates to content throughout the year;
- can customize your learning experience with relevant professional development topics, including taxes, auditing, accounting, finance, information technology, and more;
- get insights on the latest standards and trends in the accounting profession; and
- earn your credits fast with 24/7 easy online access to CPE courses.

Group pricing

If you have 5 or more people, contact one of our learning consultants regarding group discounts that can help maximize the ROI of your learning initiatives. Learn more at aicpastore.com/content/media/Training/group-training.jsp or call 800.634.6780, option 1.

Subscribe today at AICPAStore.com/CPExpress or call 888.777.7077.

Annual Webcast Pass

With our Annual Webcast Pass, you can explore a variety of topics specific to what you're interested in now — or what you'd like to try in the future. You can choose courses from outside your required subject area and expand your knowledge at no additional cost. It's professional guidance, year-round. You'll get

- professional guidance from top experts, regulators and industry leaders across major fields of study, including auditing, accounting, taxes, information technology, and more;
- learning content that encourages you to look closely at your own practice, ask questions; and make connections;
- live webcasts from one to eight hours, so you can plan your learning around your schedule;
- one year of access to more than 500 AICPA webcasts on hot topics (such as tax reform, blockchain, data analytics, and more), critical updates, and the latest standards.

Group pricing

If you have 5 or more people, contact one of our learning consultants regarding group discounts that can help maximize the ROI of your learning initiatives. Learn more at aicpastore.com/content/media/Training/group-training.jsp or call 800.634.6780, option 1.

Subscribe today at AICPAStore.com/CPExpress or call 888.777.7077.

Your strategic learning partner

Let us help prepare your staff for the future.

What is your current approach to learning? One size does not fit all. Your organization is unique, and your approach to learning and competency should be, too. But where do you start? Choose a strategic partner to help you assess competencies and gaps, design a customized learning plan, and measure and maximize the ROI of your learning and development initiatives.

We offer a wide variety of learning programs for finance professionals at every stage of their career.

AICPA Learning resources can help you:
- Create a learning culture to attract and retain talent
- Enrich staff competency and stay current on changing regulations
- Sharpen your competitive edge
- Capitalize on emerging opportunities
- Meet your goals and positively impact your bottom line
- Address CPE/CPD compliance

Flexible learning options include:
- On-site training
- Conferences
- Webcasts
- Certificate programs
- Online self-study
- Publications

An investment in learning can directly impact your bottom line. Contact an AICPA learning consultant to begin your professional development planning.

Call: 800.634.6780, option 1
Email: AICPALearning@aicpa.org